THE DESERT JOURNAL

The Desert Journal

A DIARY 1954-55

Carlo Carretto

Translated by
ALISON SWAISLAND BUCCI

ORBIS BOOKS

Maryknoll, New York 10545

271.79
Ca D

B
Carretto
Ca D

The Catholic Foreign Mission Society of America (Maryknoll) recruits and trains people for overseas missionary service. Through Orbis Books Maryknoll aims to foster the internatioal dialogue that is essential to mission. The books published, however, reflect the opinions of their authors and are not meant to represent the official position of the Society.

Originally published in Italian as *El-Abiodh: diario spirituale 1954–1955* by Cittadella Editrice, Assisi, Italy in 1990
Copyright © Cittadella Editrice, 1990

This English translation first published in Great Britain in 1992 by Fount Paperbacks, an imprint of HarperCollins*Religious*, 77–85 Fulham Palace Road, London W6 8JB

Published in the United States of America by Orbis Books, Maryknoll NY 10545

Copyright in the English translation by HarperCollins*Publishers* © 1992

Typeset by Avocet Typesetters, Bicester, Oxon
Printed in Great Britain by HarperCollins Manufacturing, Glasgow

LIBRARY OF CONGRESS CATALOGUING–IN–PUBLICATION DATA

Carretto, Carlo.
    [Abiodh, diario spirituale, 1954–1955. English]
    The desert journal / by Carlo Carretto; edited by Gian Carlo Sibilla; translated by Alison Bucci.
        p.   cm.
    ISBN 0-88344-844-0 : $9.95
        1. Carretto, Carlo – Diaries.   2. Monks – Algeria – Diaries.
3. Little Brothers of Jesus – Spiritual life.   4. Spiritual life –
Catholic Church.   5. Catholic Church – Membership.   I. Title.
BX4705.C3183A3   1992
271'.79 – dc20
[B]   92-24101
                                                                    CIP

Contents

Introduction by René Voillaume   7

Preface by Gian Carlo Sibilia   11

Biographical notes on Carlo Carretto   13

THE DIARY   17

Appendices

  1. An Address by Professor Carlo Carretto   133
  2. Charles de Foucauld – founder of
       the Little Brothers of Jesus   136
  3. The Testimony of Arturo Paoli   153
  4. Brother Milad Aïssa (1912-84)   161
  5. Testimonials   168
  6. Mario Fumagalli   172

Notes   179

Introduction

When he received his habit of the Little Brothers of Jesus on Christmas Day 1954, Carlo Carretto joined a community of twenty or so brother novices in El-Abiodh-Sidi-Cheikh. His friend, Arturo Paoli, a former assistant of Italian Catholic Action, had arrived there before him and taken the habit two months earlier, on 24 October that same year.

El-Abiodh-Sidi-Cheikh is a little oasis on the edge of the Sahara, beside the last small foothills of the Atlas Mountains, about five hundred kilometres south of the city of Oran in Western Algeria. Since the seventeenth century this oasis had been the headquarters of the Muslim confraternity of the Cheikhiyas, founded by Sidi Cheikh, a holy man and a great tribal chief. His tomb and those of his sons, simple whitewashed mausoleums topped by the domes so characteristic of the area, are venerated and visited by many pilgrims.

Here, in this centre for numerous nomadic tribes, and far off the beaten track, the Little Brothers of Jesus set up their first foundation in 1933 in an abandoned fortress, a rather isolated *bordij* in the *reg*,[1] solidly built around a courtyard with a portico which looked rather like a cloister. A big, completely white chapel, with a cupola in the style of Sidi Cheikh's *koubbas*, was built as soon as the Little Brothers settled in this place which the tribes claiming descent from Sidi Cheikh considered, in a way, to be holy ground.

Originally the Little Brothers of Jesus were devoted only to the apostolate to Islam. However, thanks to a whole series of providential events, they followed their vocation of presence, friendship and prayer, and played a part in the new approach of the Church to the plight of the working classes in France. Abbot Godin's book, *France, Terre de Mission*, the first worker-priests of the Paris Mission and, later, the Mission of France all helped to pave the way for the working Fraternity of the Brothers and Sisters of Frère Charles de Jésus. Begun between

1946 and 1947, this rapid spread of foundations in industrial areas, not only in France but in other countries too, was made possible by the large number of young people who applied to join the Fraternity after the war. Over a ten-year period there were, on average, more than fifteen to twenty novices per year, and some novitiates numbered over forty. Brother Noël Retailleau entered the Fraternity in 1935 and took his vows with the name of Milad Aïssa (or simply Milad), which means "Jesus' birth" in Arabic. During the period in question, he was in charge of the El Abiodh novitiate.

Carlo Carretto's spiritual diary is the limpid and simple record of the action of the Holy Spirit in his novice's soul. This manuscript also shows what that year of training for the religious life was like, in the severe atmosphere of the desert which stripped him spiritually, and how he discovered the intimate existence of God in his soul, under the direction of Brother Milad. I was greatly moved on reading these pages, which are imbued with the total generosity of his faith and his willingness to do the work of grace. This straightforward text does not require comment, so I merely intend to shed light on a few passages in footnotes, to help the reader understand the events that Carlo refers to.

At the end of his year of novitiate, Carlo took temporary vows with the Little Brothers of Jesus on Christmas Day 1955. Subsequently he spent time in a series of working Fraternities, especially in Berrel'Etang, and finally in Tamanrasset in the Ahaggar Mountains in the heart of the Sahara – the same place where Charles de Foucauld died in 1916. He took his perpetual vows on 15 September 1961.

In 1964 he helped found the Bindua Fraternity in the diocese of Iglesias in Sardinia. This foundation, consecrated to the evangelization of a community of miners which had completely lapsed from Christianity, was entrusted to the Little Brothers of the Gospel, a congregation recently founded as an offshoot of the Little Brothers of Jesus, and which differs from them in that their vocation is for evangelization and pastoral ministry. Carlo wrote to the Prior of the Little Brothers of Jesus from Bindua at Pentecost 1965, asking to be allowed to transfer to the Little Brothers of the Gospel.

After his admission to the Fraternity of the Gospel as a perpetual professed religious, he helped until the following year, 1966, in the founding of the Fraternity of St Jerome in Spello. He stayed in this Fraternity until his death in 1988, except for two periods spent at the Béni Abbès Fraternity in the Algerian Sahara, which Frère Charles de Jésus had chosen for his hermitage in 1901. Brother Carlo spent two years there, from 1968 to 1970, and then he went back for a shorter visit in 1972.

All who ever knew and loved Brother Carlo, all those who have gained something from him through his writings and, above all, during retreats in Spello, which he inspired with his glowing faith and the immense cordiality of his fraternal welcome, will be delighted to discover the source of his life of intimacy with Jesus, in this diary. The fruitfulness of his ministry of the word – a ministry he was consecrated to with the order of deaconship in January 1969 – was the direct result of his self-abnegation and his rich and varied earlier career. He agreed to make this act of renunciation in answer to God's call during his novitiate in the desert, and in obedience to his vocation as a Little Brother and follower of Frère Charles de Jésus. This diary is a faithful account of that experience.

Father René Voillaume
Cépie, 15 August 1990

Preface

One night towards the end of November 1969, at El-Abiodh, Brother Carlo told us about this diary and promised to give it to us. Brother Milad and Brother Ermete were with us as we came out of the chapel after the adoration of the Eucharist, and we stopped to admire a sky full of stars. Anyone who knows the desert is familiar with the splendour and enchantment of the Saharan sky!

Then Brother Carlo linked arms with us and took us for a stroll in the garden where we also paid a visit to the small cemetery. It was a long night, because Carlo got carried away by his memories of the novitiate. He told us the same things we were later to find in his diary, which is now being published.

From time to time Brother Carlo stopped to compare the course of his novitiate with what came afterwards, during his life as a religious. In order to convince us that everything is always the work of God, and to make us understand how surprising he found that, he told us for the first time about an audience he had had with Pope John XXIII. The Pope came forward to meet him, and stopping him almost before he could come in, said:

"Professor, I have thought of you a great deal this morning and I have already prayed for you. Tell me, Professor, would you ever have imagined you would become a religious?"

Carlo said no, and John XXIII walked towards his chair saying to himself, "Nor me, nor me . . . that I would become Pope! . . ."

Naturally, Brother Carlo remarked to the Pope that one could hardly compare the two things, but he went on:

"No, no, it's exactly the same thing, dear Professor. You always end up where you would never have dreamed of being. But . . . *voluntas Dei, pax nostra.*"

*

After some months in Rome we sorted through Brother Carlo's writings, which he enlivened with anecdotes, but in the end, despite our pleading and attempts to stop him, most of them went on the bonfire. All that was saved were a few letters, the promised diary of a novitiate and another big diary which Brother Carlo let us keep because it contained, among other things, some of his reflections on the Oratory, a project which in his view was being re-created in the emergent Comunità Jesus Caritas.

There were other occasions on which writings received and sent by Brother Carlo were burned. Only during his last years did he relent and of his own initiative give us material and authorize his relatives to give us what was left (very little, to tell the truth) in the possession of the family.

Therefore the editors would like to thank the Carretto-Turchi family, and to express our gratitude to the Marseilles secretariat of the Little Brothers of Jesus and to our Brother and friend Jean-François Nothomb, for all the information he has given us. A special thank-you is due to Father René Voillaume.

As in *Letters to Dolcidia*, we have added footnotes to give a picture of Charles de Foucauld's Fraternity – the spiritual family which made such a profound impression on Brother Carlo.

Appendix 2 contains first-hand accounts of the founding and growth of the Little Brothers of Jesus. Some of these pieces have been shortened, but the content of the originals has been respected and most of the texts are dated; the vocabulary has been preserved, though today the wording might be different.

So Brother Carlo is still with us through his writings, although now he has the added advantage of being able to embellish his words with perpetual intercessory prayer to his and our "beloved brother and Lord, Jesus".

Gian Carlo Sibilia

As far as possible the text of the diary has been left in its original form. Brother Carlo's underlinings are represented by italics. In a few places square brackets are used to indicate the omission of things which, for the present, must remain confidential. Scripture references have been added in those cases where they were left out in the original manuscript.

Biographical Notes on Carlo Carretto

Carlo Carretto was born in Alessandria on 2 April 1910, but soon afterwards the family moved, first to Moncalieri and then to Turin. He received a profoundly religious education within the family, which he continued at the Salesian Oratory of the Crocetta. At the age of eighteen he became a primary school teacher and, after taking a degree in history and philosophy, he won a competitive examination for a post of junior school headmaster in Sardinia. Due to clashes with the Fascist regime he was sent back to Piedmont and, having refused to take the oath of fealty to the Republic of Salò, he was struck from the register of headmasters and placed under surveillance.

During those years he went from being a militant member of the Turin branch of Azione Cattolica Giovanile (Catholic Action for Youth) to taking over the management of Catholic Action for Northern Italy, and he inaugurated many apostolic projects.

In 1945 he was called to Rome by Pope Pius XII and Luigi Gedda to set up the Association of Catholic Teachers. In 1946 he became director of the GIAC (Gioventù Italiana d'Azione Cattolica – Italian Youth for Catholic Action), and soon afterwards he founded the Bureau International de la Jeunesse Catholique.

He made a charismatic president of the GIAC. In 1948 he summoned more than three hundred thousand young people – the famous *baschi verdi* or "green berets" – to Rome to celebrate Catholic Action's eightieth anniversary.

In 1953 controversy broke out in Catholic circles over involvement in politics, and Carlo had to resign as director of the GIAC. However, with Lazzati, La Pira and Gonella, he still continued to seek new outlets for the concerned Catholic laity.

God was lying in wait for him and called him to the religious life, and on 8 December 1954 Carlo set off to begin his novitiate with the

Little Brothers of Jesus in the Algerian Sahara. There followed ten long years of profound spiritual experience made up of silence, prayer and work. *Lettere dal Deserto* told the story of this pilgrimage to many readers in Italy and all over the world.

He returned to Europe and, after spending periods in a number of Fraternities, he settled in Spello, Umbria, at the end of 1965. From that moment the Fraternity of the Little Brothers assumed a role in the Italian Church which grew increasingly important over the years. Thousands of people, especially the young, found a place of welcome, prayer and silence there. For twenty years Carlo was the leading spirit of all this, with his teaching and his writings, which proliferated and were translated into many languages.

On 4 October 1988, the Feast Day of St Francis of Assisi, after some years of ill health, in his small cell at Spello he passed on to Eternal Life in an atmosphere of great pascal joy, shared by the hundreds of people who had come flocking from all parts of Italy and from abroad to be with him.

The Diary: 1954

DECEMBER 1954

The Feast of the Immaculate Conception
I set out[1] from Termini at 20.20. Many dear friends came to see me off. I am leaving my past – good and bad at one and the same time – behind to go to the desert. Liliana wrote to me that I must forget everything,[2] and in a way she is right. I hoped he would come [. . .], but he didn't. Ah well! He doesn't understand these gestures any more. But perhaps I'm the one who's wrong.

9 December
We got to Marseilles three hours late. I say "we" because Poldo and Nino[3] were with me. We went straight to the Fraternity in the pouring rain, where Frère Henry[4] in his great goodness made us welcome. We made plans to visit Saint-Maximin[5] and Berre[6] tomorrow. In the evening we went to La Cappellette[7] and, naturally, we were very favourably impressed.

10 December
We went to Saint-Maximin, where the Little Brothers study. An unforgettable visit. There is great unity of thought and action and they all set a shining example. Simplicity, serenity, poverty and peace reign supreme. These young men don't appear to have any problems! To Berre in the evening.

11 December
I am aboard the boat for Oran.[8] It is a fine French vessel of around ten thousand tons, called the *Sidi Bel Abbes*. After yesterday's rain the sun is shining brightly, which promises an excellent crossing. I said goodbye to Nino and Poldo at customs, as they are returning to Rome. I am going up on deck to pray.

The *Sidi Bel Abbes* cast off at eleven o'clock. Lunch with a French colonialist from Algeria. His conversation gives one an inkling of a dramatic past which has left hair caught in the comb of time . . . The weather is good. I shall use the time to write the last letters and to think. I recited vespers to a stupendous sea and was reduced to tears of joy. During the evening the sea became calm and I was able to write at the desk. I wrote to [. . .], thinking of the strength of his love. If only he could purify it, there would be nothing that boy could not do. Tomorrow morning I shall see Africa.

12 December
Dawn over the sea – St Augustine's sea.

At 13.30 the *Bel Abbes* docked in the port of Oran. It is a little windy and the sky is clouded over, but nonetheless this beautiful Algerian city has made an excellent impression on me. I sought out the local Fraternity. I went on a brief excursion to Santa Cruz,[9] which reminded me of the former Spanish rulers and of the colony still there in the city. I bought a ticket for my onward journey and dined in a small restaurant with the local Little Brothers.

13 December
At dawn I set off for the interior by coach. We crossed the whole of the Algerian coastal strip, which is every bit as beautiful as the loveliest Mediterranean scenery, and arrived in Saïda[10] at about ten o'clock.

An hour's rest, a change of coaches and off again towards the South. Along the way the vines gradually became less frequent and the cold grew more intense. The grasslands of the plateau appeared. We reached Géryville,[11] the last town of any size, close to four in the afternoon. As arranged, I went to the Mission of the White Fathers.[12] I spent the night in the Mission itself in a humble bed near a lit stove. The weather is threatening and I am worried that I won't be able to leave because the roads may become impassable.

14 December

The night brought stars and dry weather: we can leave. I confess to having prayed for this – I am so eager to get there. The sun is splendid, but the cold is intense. A novel experience, quite unknown to Europeans. The landscape becomes increasingly arid on this plateau, which is covered with tufts of esparto grass and inhabited by poor people who scratch a living from sheep-farming. The further one goes, the more the scenery changes and the grassland gives way to the desert. The last stop before El-Abiodh is already in the desert. At three o'clock, far away in the distance the white speck of El-Abiodh appears.[13] We're there! The first stage is over: I have tears in my eyes.

My first encounter with this oasis of peace was somewhat emotional. I espied Don Arturo[14] dressed like a simple workman, utterly cheerful and serene. With a hasty look round the premises, I took stock of my surroundings. Poverty rules supreme everywhere, and it is obvious what inspiration lies behind it. It isn't easy to speak of this right away, so I shall wait till later, when I have a clearer idea of things.

I met Fr Voillaume[15] for the first time – a true giant spiritually and, I might add, physically – and Fr Milad,[16] the Master of Novices, of whom there are about forty.[17] They all profess great scorn for conventions, elegance and comfort. It is immediately apparent that this is something of a game, but a constructive one nonetheless: joy, work, prayer, simplicity and reciprocal love abound. I am happy.

17 December

I am afraid I won't be allowed to begin my novitiate at Christmas. It is a very simple, ordinary thing, but it saddens me. Therefore it is a very black day, accompanied by a total aridity of mind and heart. In other words, one of the blackest days of recent times.

18 December

How changeable is the heart of man, especially when the man is called Carlo. Yesterday I was so sad, and yet today I am one of the happiest people on earth. At dawn Fr Milad took me to one side to tell me that I can become a novice at Christmas. Perhaps it was the news, pehaps the worship, perhaps the singing, but whatever it was, I wept for joy.

I saw the precious pearl and I would not exchange it for all the gold in the world. I saw my path and I would not change it for any other. The ideal of the Little Brother shone before me as the sum of all things suffered, believed, experienced and understood. Now I must prepare myself.

19 December

My first Sunday in the novitiate. During the hour of adoration I worked out a formula which I intend to give here because I feel it might be useful.

Recite the Miserere (psalm 50), making an excursus on men and their sins.

Recite the Te Deum or the Benedictus (Luke 1:68–79) while meditating on the different parts of the world – their beauty and the people who live there.

At the end I made up my mind to cure my basic malady, which is selfishness, by practising charity and always taking something of my own and putting it in Gelsomina's mess tin.[18] We shall see.

20 December

I have been trying to come up with some guidelines for becoming a good novice. Since, in this case, I will have to overcome my notorious gift for fooling others and for superficiality, I think a good method would be to judge myself by the same yardstick I would apply to another novice who has the same faults as me and who is up to the same tricks as me. I think this is what I would suggest:

1. I'd like him to leap straight out of bed in the morning.
2. I'd like him to obey the spirit of the rule and not just the letter. (Sincerity.)
3. At table he should always take less rather than more.
4. At work he should concentrate on the true nature of things, and

not merely on their outward form just to make himself look good and clever.

5. Utter truthfulness in conversation, especially when talking about the past.

6. He should study the true and practical meaning of poverty.

This evening Fr Voillaume spoke about prayer again.

There are two parties to this fundamental act: God and man.

God expects us: this is a comforting truth. God encourages us. He wants us to pray. Without him we could do nothing at all.

We, humankind, are on the other end, of course. It is not easy to pray, because true prayer takes true faith. But we have to make the effort and plunge in bravely, in complete trust. We must, and we can, become men of prayer. Perhaps we can begin by helping ourselves along with some text from the Scriptures and with formulae, but above all with the patient and calm repetition of the "Pater". Then the rest will follow, until faith and love alone are needed.

Good night.

22 December

"Whoever does not receive the kingdom of God as a little child will never enter it" (Mark 10:15). The natural progression of life is from childhood to old age. On the contrary, the Kingdom of God within us goes from the age of an old man to the childhood of the spiritually renewed man. This calls for two yardsticks: during the natural course of life one grows in prudence, wisdom and responsibility; but in spiritual life one grows in childlikeness, simplicity, impulsiveness, joy, clarity and unity of purpose.

Jesus used the child as a symbol.

Chastity is the fate of all people. After the second coming of Christ there will no longer be bridegrooms or brides, but all shall be like the angels in Heaven. Chastity on earth simply anticipates that condition. However, we still have to solve the problem of fertility which is inherent in the mystery of man and woman. Is it possible for Christ to take this potential away from his dear ones? Impossible: fertility will be transformed, not taken away.

At this point it is essential to reflect on the role played by the chaste person in Christ's fruitful work in the world.

23 December

Tomorrow is Christmas Eve. The Master of Novices has announced that I will be given my habit at Christmas. This is very important to me. I must begin, for there is a lot to be done in my poor soul and I must work hard at it. I must learn! . . . what a lot I have to learn! . . . it is useless to list it all. I had better put myself in the hands of the Holy Redeemer, my Lord Jesus. He brought me here: *he will complete the gift.*

This evening Fr Milad read the passage about the birth of Jesus. Then he commented on the text, stressing Jesus' poverty: a simple poverty, of the people, without excesses. It was natural for a poor family not to find a place to stay in Bethlehem. It was natural for a poor man to look for a cave. Whereas John's poverty has something *éclatante* about it, that of Jesus is ordinary. It is simple, of the people, genuine. It is the natural example for the Fraternity to follow, and an example for each Little Brother. I must remember the poverty of my family in Moncalieri.[19] That is what I must return to.

Christmas Eve

Tomorrow I will receive the habit of a Little Brother.

I am going to copy down here the questions Fr Voillaume will ask before accepting me as a novice.

Q. Frère, que demandes-tu?
A. Je demande à être admis parmi les Petits Frères de Jésus.
Q. Es-tu prêt, à cause de l'Evangile de Jésus, à vivre non seulement pauvrement, sans rien posséder, mais à accepter aussi la condition des pauvres obligés à travailler pour vivre, en accomplissement de la loi divine?
A. Je désire sincèrement être pauvre à cause de Jésus et de l'Evangile.

Q. Es-tu décidé à prendre l'habitude d'obéir de bon coeur à Dieu et aux hommes qui ont le pouvoir de te commander en son nom parce que Jésus s'est fair obéissant jusqu'à la mort, et que tu veux travailler avec lui à la rédemption de tes frères?

A. Je désire vraiment me soumettre à toute obéissance, à cause de Jésus et du salut de mes frères.

Q. Es-tu décidé à prier chaque jour avec foi et courage, en union avec l'Eucharistie, et à persévérer malgré les difficultés, confiant dans les promesses de Jésus sur la prière?

A. Je le promets à Jésus en son sacrement, et je lui demanderai de m'aider.

Q. Es-tu prêt, à l'exemple du Frère Charles de Jésus, ton guide et ton soutien, à tout sacrifier et à aller partout où l'obéissance t'enverra?

A. Je désire aimer tout homme sans me décourager, confiant pour cela en la force de l'amour de Jésus, maître de l'impossible.[20]

It is almost Christmas. This is the second time I have spent it away from home. The first time was in Bethlehem,[21] and the second is here in El-Aboidh. I don't feel particularly homesick, for Jesus is sparing me the deeper sorrows. He knows that I am weak, very weak.

At six we attended general chapter. Each of us confessed his sins before the whole community. It is a beautiful thing, but terribly difficult, because we all tend to overdo it. I want to accuse myself of just one thing: of not loving the Lord as I ought. This is the heart of the problem. If I can achieve a powerful love for God, all the rest will fall into place. Otherwise it is pointless to single out details which are meaningless without love, the prime mover.

But who will give me love for God? Of course, he alone has this power, and with humility and determination I shall ask him to grant it this night, which I am spending away from home for his sake.

I am willing to strip myself of everything, even to die, but I want his love. Without him I feel a terrifying emptiness, a void, an unbearable sadness. How true it is that man is made for God! Nothing in this world attracts me any more, and I have yet to put down roots in God. It is almost like hanging in mid-air.

God help me. *I have faith in you* and you know it. I believed you would free me from the bonds of death. I believed you would solve the problem my will could no longer cope with. My act of faith was my only show of strength, and you came. Thank you, O Lord! Now finish the job; you do it, don't trust me, gather me to you, give me back the joy of First Love. Do you remember when you called to me in the desert of my youth? I was twenty-three then[22] and you held me in your arms like a bride. Give me back that joy. I am sure you have forgiven my past, because you said so in Jeremiah: "Could a married woman who has been unfaithful to her husband go back to him, polluted and adulterous? You have given yourselves to many. But come back to the Lord and he will take you back on the old terms and establish an everlasting pact with you" (cf. Jeremiah 3:1). How sweet all this is, Lord, and how it reveals the depth of your love for us!

So tonight I want to repeat my act of faith. *Lord, I believe in your love. You expended great power to bring me here. You will complete your gift by gathering me to you, by granting me the gift your love requires of you and love for the poor, which means all mankind.*

I asked Milad for some inspiring thoughts for my novitiate. He told me: "Seek for the substance by observing the form. Light and heat will come naturally."

St Stephen's Day

Yesterday evening Fr Voillaume gave a talk and urged us to strive for a spirit of spiritual infancy. He cited the evangelical concept of the child, which is how we must be in relation to God. Let us take a look at some features of this childhood. The child believes in its father, is not afraid with him there and trusts him blindly. It doesn't worry about what it will eat tomorrow because it knows he is there. This immense, radical faith, this complete surrender of self, this simplicity with which the child looks up to its father, has to be my attitude to God. There is no surer way. All faith works to this end. Otherwise, Jesus says, we shall never enter the Kingdom of Heaven (cf. Mark 10:15). Indeed, what would Mary have done and thought if she had not been guided by the spiritual childhood given her by faith? Would she have understood the mystery of Jesus' birth? Would she have accepted the incomprehensible massacre of the innocents? How could the Almighty not intervene, though he performed a miracle in warning Joseph to flee? There's no point in going on, because human-divine life is so much of a mystery that only faith accepted with the simplicity of a child can solve it. *This is my way.*

So, I have become a *Little Brother of Jesus*. This is the fitting title for a Christian and the proper relationship to have with Jesus. This relationship reinforces the other relationship, with the Father. I am a son of the Father, a member of his family by virtue of the blood of his firstborn, Jesus. And what about the relationship with the Holy Spirit? It seems to me that the most apt analogy – in emulation of the Virgin – is that of the bride. The Holy Spirit consists entirely of God's love; it is the very love which binds the Father to the Son. It is the love which creates and sanctifies. Therefore, it is the love of God which seeks that love whose symbol is marriage. Thus the love of God is my Bridegroom and I must immerse myself, lose myself, rejoice and find consolation in this love tomorrow.

And this is where my potential fruitfulness comes from – this ineffable relationship with love.

Viens Esprit Créateur. My sweet Bridegroom, because the bride springs from the bridegroom's rib.

Visite les esprits des tiens. Your fervour seeks us out because you are the passionate lover.

Remplis de célestes grâces. What do you bring with your coming? Everything. Indeed, when you are present in the soul, what more could possibly be desired? Nothing, because you are everything, everything that totally satisfies and fulfils.

Les coeurs que tu as créés. These hearts are yours, they belong to you by virtue of their very purpose, they are driven to you, you alone can satisfy them, Spirit of Creation.

Toi qui es appelé Paraclet. Don du Dieu très-haut. Love is not the most beautiful gift; it is the giving of self with charity and in the most perfect imitation of God.

Source vivante, feu, amour. Behold the Bridegroom – living waters in the thirsty desert, all things bestowed on Creation, air to the lungs, light to the shadows; everything, everything. And more, he is like fire, like undying love. Sweet, sweet Bridegroom!

C'est toi l'Esprit aux sept dons: Wisdom – Intellect – Counsel – Strength – Knowledge – Pity – Fear of God.

Le doigt de la droite paternelle. What is the function of the raised finger on God's right hand? It points the way, it is the beacon to keep in view when making decisions.

C'est toi le vrai promis du Père. Can there be a better promise of love than that of a bridegroom to his bride, or a lover to his loved one?

Qui arrichis notre langue. All is silent without you, but with you our tongues are loosened and we talk and talk. The Prophets talk, John talks, Jesus talks, the Church talks, the Saints talk.

Allume la lumière en nos sens. Our poor senses, obscured by Adam's taint! But you love, illuminate, clarify and exhort.

Verse l'amour dans nos coeurs. Just so, because otherwise it is impossible to love God and mankind.

Ce qu'il y a d'infirme en nos corps. Affirme-le par constante vigueur. It is your task, sweet physician of the soul, restorer of the fallen, our sanctifier.

Repousse l'ennemi loin de nous. Donne-nous bien vite la paix. It is you, Love, who protects your bride, who guides her and who leads her through the desert, towards the promised land, towards peace.

"Peace!" That is the gift of Love, the greatest gift promised by Jesus in Bethlehem.

Pour que ainsi, marchant à ta suite, nous évitions tous ce qui nuit. The guide has been chosen – Love – the heavenly Bridegroom, the End, the All. With childlike spirit run where he guides you, let him lead you; seek out the unknown, perceive in all that is not yours a definite instruction from him. Trust blindly and walk. He will never let you down, for it is impossible for him to neglect you, not love you, not think of you. Let him lead you: *have faith.*

God the Father, God the Son, God the Holy Ghost, I love you, I accept your guidance, I put myself in your hands in all things, now and forever. Amen.

The childlike spirit called for by God also has a good deal to do with a person's attitude to his own future. A child is trusting; it doesn't make plans, since it knows its father is there. It doesn't worry about what it will eat for it knows its father is there. It doesn't fear journeys as long as he is there. This is true surrender of self, humble surrender, serene surrender into the hands of one who is all-powerful, all-knowing and all-caring.

Another feature of this spirit is how small it is. A child knows how small it is and is aware that it is of little importance and knows little. It does not trouble itself with irrelevant relationships. *It does not count*, as if it did not exist. Who takes care of it? Whose job is it to take care of it? It is never the focus of interest, and that is just the way things are. Moreover, the childlike spirit *is faith*. It believes, it lives by faith.

What is more, it is poor – pure – a lover of justice and of the triumph of innocence. *In other words, it has no trouble in accepting the laws of the Kingdom: the Beatitudes.* Let us read them again with a child in mind.

> Blessed are the poor in spirit,
> for theirs is the kingdom of heaven.
> Blessed are those who mourn,
> for they will be comforted.
> Blessed are the meek,
> for they will inherit the earth.
> Blessed are those who hunger
> and thirst for righteousness,
> for they will be filled.
> Blessed are the merciful,
> for they will receive mercy.
> Blessed are the pure in heart,
> for they will see God.
> Blessed are the peacemakers,
> for they will be called children of God.
>
> (Matthew 5:3-9)

Is a child not poor, meek, merciful, pacific and pure?

Does it not mourn? Does it not thirst after righteousness and knowledge?

Truly the symbol chosen by Jesus is perfect.

29 December

This morning I meditated on my relationship with my brother Jesus, especially with regard to what he said about himself. Here is a list of these references:

I am the good shepherd (John 10:11).

I am the light of the world (John 8:12).

I am the way, and the truth, and the life (John 14:6).

I am among you as one who serves (Luke 22:27).

The Son of Man is Lord of the sabbath (Matthew 12:8).

God did not sent the Son into the world to condemn the world, but in order that the world might be saved through him (John 3:17).

I am the resurrection (John 11:25).

My words will not pass away (Mark 13:31).

My food is to do the will of him who sent me (John 4:34).

I am the bread of life (John 6:35).

Whoever believes has eternal life (John 6:47).

In the beginning was the Word . . . and the Word was God (John 1:1).

I do not seek my own glory (John 8:50).

Before Abraham was, I am (John 8:58).

I am the gate (John 10:9).

The Father and I are one (John 10.30).

And I, when I am lifted up from the earth, will draw all people to myself (John 12:32).

I have set you an example (John 13:15).

I will not leave you orphaned (John 14:18).

I am the true vine, and my Father is the vinegrower (John 15:1).

I am the vine, you are the branches (John 15:5).

I do not call you servants any longer . . . but I have called you friends (John 15:15).

I came from the Father, and have come into the world; again, I am leaving the world and am going to the Father (John 16:28).

I am asking on their behalf (John 17:9).

I am a king (John 18:37).

Learn from me; for I am gentle and humble in heart (Matthew 11:29).

The Son of Man has nowhere to lay his head (Luke 9:58).

I am with you always, to the end of the age (Matthew 28:20).

30 December

Love is the key to all the mysteries of Christianity. Without it the precious caskets of Jesus' thought cannot be unlocked. It is the theme of the beatitudes and the very life of God. How could chastity be understood without love? And what does poverty become if it is not motivated by love for God and one's neighbour? A senseless, ineffectual thing. Carlo, you must accept this as your vocation and call on love in all difficulties of thought or deed.

31 December

An incontrovertible act of faith which you must adopt is: he knows, he will guide you, he will keep faith. He will reveal himself, he will complete the task which has been begun.

Meanwhile here we are on St Sylvester's Day. 1954 is on its way out, taking all its old, so very old, things with it, and the only new thing about the year arriving tonight is that I have joined the Little Brothers. If I were to sum up this past year it would be an endless list of negative things. I can truly say that I sank to the depths, where one lies motionless like the hulks of wrecked ships. I am certain of this, and I will be able to draw on this certainty without hesitation in the future when trials come my way. I would have died of spiritual consumption if I had stayed in the world. Perhaps I won't make it even on the road I have chosen because the disease has struck to the heart, but I believe that here the healing virtue of Almighty God must shine through. If he has brought me here he must still have hope for me. I shall stumble but I am counting above all on him. This morning I made this absolute act of faith and I intend to repeat it often. In summing up the situation to date I can say:

1. *I believe the Lord will lead me to him as if I were a sheep*, to be with him, to love only him, to renew the ancient pact.
2. *I believe he will teach me to pray.*
3. *I shall try to achieve spiritual childhood, striving above all for love.* To help make this easier I shall improve my relationships with:
     Jesus the brother
     the Father
     the Holy Spirit, the Bridegroom.
4. I shall try to live the beatitudes with good will and with maximum receptiveness to the action of the Holy Spirit.
5. I shall always try to *be* and not to *seem*, in truth and in freedom.
6. I shall pit all my strength against my selfishness because it is an obstacle to the rule of love I have chosen as my vocation and as my natural spiritual attitude.

The Diary: 1955

2 January

The name of Jesus

Jesu decus angelicum
In aure dulce canticum
In ore mel mirificum
In corde nectar caelicum.[1]

This morning I summed up my relationships with the Three Divine Persons under three headings:

Our Father
Sweet Jesus, my brother
Holy Spirit, fons vitae, ignis, charitas.[2]

and above all, trust, trust, trust. If these relationships are to be genuine, the first attitude of the soul must be that of absolute certainty. The Three Divine Persons will complete the gift; they will teach me how to pray and the meaning of the beatitudes. They will divulge their prime attribute to me: love, charity. That is the faith I must have.

3 January

I am going to write about two thoughts today. The first concerns trust in God and the second charity. As I want to learn to perceive God's will working in me, I shall accept with particular interest all those things which are not thought of or organized by me. When faced with a choice *I shall have others choose for me* if possible.

Regarding charity, I must make an effort to get away from myself as much as possible. The more I think of others, the more I shall get used to not thinking of myself. The more I forget myself, the better things will go for me.

Your Kingdom Come

Where there is hate, let there be your love
Where there is war, let there be peace
Where there is uncleanness, let there be purity
Where there is lust, let there be chastity
Where there is violence, let there be meekness
Where there is vengeance, let there be forgiveness
Where there is wealth, let there be charity
Where there is poverty, let there be joyful acceptance
Where there is terror, let there be tranquillity
Where there is sadness, let there be rejoicing
Where there is fear of death, let there be faith
Where there is desperation, let there be peace
Where there is sin, let there be grace
Where there is half-heartedness, let there be fervour
Where there is selfishness, let there be giving
Where there is calculation, let there be generosity
Where there is atheism, let there be adoration
Where there is darkness, let there be light
Where there is lewdness, let there be virginity
Where there is self-abasement, let there be strength of character
Where a child rebels, let there be submission
Where the father is unworthy, let there be your discipline
Where there is sadness, let there be joy
Where there is emptiness, let it be filled
Where there is death, let there be life
Where there is exploitation, let there be correctness
Where there is theft, let there be giving
Where there is arrogance, let there be humility
Where there is power, let there be caring
Where there is communism, let there be a spirit of community
Where there is racism, let there be catholicism
Your Kingdom come.

A problem which has often worried me concerns the resistance the soul puts up to grace. I am making a note of those passages in the gospels containing instructions.

"When anyone hears the word of the kingdom and does not understand, the evil one comes and snatches away what is sown in the heart; this is what was sown on the path. As for what was sown on rocky ground, this is the one who hears the word and immediately receives it with joy; yet such a person has no root, but endures only for a while, and when trouble or persecution arises on account of the word, that person immediately falls away. As for what was sown among thorns, this is the one who hears the word, but the cares of the world, and the lures of wealth choke the word, and it yields nothing" (Matthew 13:19–22).

Lack of faith – interference from the devil – inattention – superficiality – wealth – the pleasures of life. There we have a preliminary list drawn up by Jesus himself. And then:

"If any want to become my followers, let them deny themselves and take up their cross daily and follow me" (Luke 9:23).

". . . you have hidden these things from the wise and intelligent . . ." (Luke 10:21).

"Martha, Martha, you are worried and distracted by many things" (Luke 10:41).

"The eye is the lamp of the body. So, if your eye is healthy, your whole body will be full of light" (Matthew 6:22).

"Take care! Be on your guard against all kinds of greed" (Luke 12:15).

". . . strive first for the kingdom of God, and his righteousness, and all these things will be given to you as well" (Matthew 6:33).

". . . except you repent, you will all perish as they did" (Luke 13:3).

"No one can serve two masters" (Matthew 6:24).

"How hard it is for those who have wealth to enter the kingdom of God!" (Luke 18:24).

". . . whosoever would become great among you, shall be your minister: but whosoever wishes to become great among you, must be your servant" (Mark 10:43-44).

Lack of self-denial, human caution, an impure eye, greed, worldliness, refusal to repent, duplicity, riches and pride – all these feature in this further list of things which stand in the way of spiritual advancement.

Now let's see where John lays the stress:

". . . and his own people did not accept him" (1:11).

"Anyone who hears my word and believes him who sent me has eternal life" (5:24).

"How can you believe when you accept glory from one another and do not seek the glory that comes from the one who alone is God?" (5:44).

"Whoever believes in the Son has eternal life" (3:36).

"Let the one who believes in me drink . . . out of the believer's heart shall flow rivers of living water" (7:38).

"If you continue in my word you are truly my disciples; and you will know the truth, and the truth will make you free" (8:31-32).

"I am the light of the world. Whoever follows me will never walk in darkness" (8:12).

"If you love me, you will keep my commandments" (14:15).

"They who have my commandments and keep them are those who love me; and those who love me will be loved by my Father, and I will love them and reveal myself to them" (14:21).

"Abide in me as I abide in you" (15:4).

"This is my commandment, that you love one another as I have loved you" (15:12).

It is clear that for John the crux of the matter is: "listen to the word of the Lord". To listen to and put into practice the teaching of Jesus is the high road which leads to the Lord.

Let's have a look at Matthew:

". . . unless your righteousness exceeds that of the scribes and Pharisees, you will never enter the kingdom of heaven" (5:20).

"Love your enemies" (5:44).

"Beware of practising your piety before others" (6:1).

"Do not store up for yourselves treasures on earth" (6:19).

"Ask, and it will be given you" (7:7).

". . . In everything do to others as you would have them do to you" (7:12).

"Those who find their life will lose it, and those who lose their life for my sake will find it" (10:39).

". . . learn from me; for I am gentle and humble in heart" (11:29).

"If you have faith the size of a mustard seed, you will say to this mountain . . ." (17:20).

"Unless you change and become like children . . ." (18:3).

"If you wish to be perfect . . ." (19:21).

"Whatever you ask for in prayer with faith, you will receive" (21:22).

"For I was hungry and you gave me no food" (25:42).

Matthew too stresses the need to act, accomplish, give and be. It seems to me, then, that the answer is very clear: one makes no progress in one's spiritual life because of not *doing*, not *being*, not *accomplishing*. We content ourselves with saying, "Lord, Lord," but that's not enough, and he said as much. So for a person asking, "Why am I not making progress? And yet I pray, I take communion . . ." there is only one answer: "Have you given to the poor? Do you practise self-denial? How deep is your faith? Have you become a child again? How just are you? Where are your treasures stored?

That goes for me too.

It is a question of doing and not just thinking. By doing, a new reality is created, and on that one another, and so on.

The Eve of Epiphany

A magnificent adoration tonight. I must meditate on the Eucharistic mystery, which is so closely tied in with the silence of God and the hidden life of Jesus.

Epiphany

"I am the Lord, and there is no other; besides me there is no God" (Isaiah 45:5).

"Does the clay say to the one who fashions it, 'What are you making?' . . . Woe to anyone who says to a father, 'What are you begetting?', or to a woman, 'With what are you in labour?' " (Isaiah 45:9–10).

"Truly you are a God who hides himself, O God of Israel, the Saviour." . . . The Lord who created the heavens . . . and formed the earth did not create *chaos* . . . (Isaiah 45:15,18).

"I am the Lord . . . I did not speak in secret, in a land of darkness; I did not say to the offspring of Jacob, '*Seek me in chaos*': I the Lord speak the truth, I declare what is right" (Isaiah 45:18–19).

". . . we will come to them and make our home with them" (John 14:23).

"I . . . will reveal myself to them" (John 14:21).

"Do not be afraid, little flock" (Luke 12:32).

". . . apart from me you can do nothing" (John 15:5).

"He will give you another Advocate" (John 14:16).

"I desire that those also, whom you have given me, may be with me where I am" (John 17:24).

"Sanctify them in the truth" (John 17:17).

What can these impressive texts be saying if not this: "I, the God of Israel, will be with you, I will not forget you and I will sanctify you."

It is time, therefore, to give up the ridiculous notion that it is we who sanctify ourselves! God and nobody else can do it, that's for sure. And the conclusion is very simple: an act of complete and unconditional renunciation is the very least you can do.

A thought. Driven from Bethlehem by Herod's cruelty, Jesus took the road to Egypt which his people had once travelled in the opposite direction, impelled by God's love: ". . . and his own people did not accept him" (John 1:11), and not only that, but the heedless hounded

God along the same road that had been travelled by their ancestors, thanks to his infinite mercy.

Jesus!

8 January

God, I give you my will, I give you my heart, I give you all I have.

This evening I felt the meaning of poverty, obedience and consecration deeply for the first time.

Thy will be done. God's will is a reality. It created the world, it decreed redemption, it envisaged the glorification of humanity by its sublime plan of identification with Christ in his ascension to Heaven and his assumption of his divinity. The will of God not only laid down the great plans, but to further their aims it also tailored the little ones, the tiniest details, since nothing can escape its wisdom and its power.

Therefore God's will is present everywhere, in every situation, in each decision taken by man, just as it is present in the laws of instinct and nature which govern all creation. This observation is fundamental because God's will endows the world with life. The world is always present in his thoughts; indeed it is ruled by his decree of love, truth and goodness. So he is present in me and he acts by urging my will to accept his, which is ever purer, greater and more lucid.

That being settled, I feel it is of paramount importance to my soul to accept his will with *an act of total surrender* right from the start, and at the same time to strive to acquire the habit of thinking of, seeing and accepting his will in every aspect of my life.

That is what I meant to say yesterday evening when, perhaps for the first time, I submitted my will to the will of God.

Obedience has to be seen in this light.

He, not other people, must be obeyed. God is to be seen in man, and God alone. And since nothing escapes his supreme, infinite, omnipotent, loving will, it is a great thing to learn to place one's trust in the whole canvas of human and natural events with docility, as being the manifestation of the divine will, and to try and resist easy temptations. "But what can God's will have to do with these day-to-day events?" "No leaf falls if God does not will it." In the light of these observations this Christian proverb is seen to be true. Therefore yesterday evening's thought, "God, I give you my will", is right.

And I give you my heart; the very essence of consecration. It is the attitude of the soul embodied so clearly in the ancient law: I took you back, you must be faithful to me. You must not prostitute yourself with false and lying gods – I am all you need – you are mine – I am your greatest love – I love you – you are mine.

And lastly, poverty.

It is achieved by giving everything of mine to God: *Omnia mea tua sunt*[3] (Luke 15:31).

Even when you have absolutely nothing left, one look at the poorest people in the world will show you that you still have more than they.

Where does it lead? To the nakedness of Calvary.

God grant me this strength of spirit.

12 January
The silence of Nazareth!

For thirty years no one knew who Jesus was! Never has a secret been kept so well! *Deus absconditus*[4] (Isaiah 45:15). On the cross, as in the Eucharist.

14 January
Yesterday evening Brother Milad said some very beautiful things about this text from St Matthew's Gospel: "Therefore ask the Lord of the harvest to send out labourers into his harvest" (9:38). Above all *pray*. Then *be poor* ("Take no gold . . .", 10:19).

"Whatever town or village you enter, find out who in it is worthy . . ." (10:11). The action of the apostle is *preceded* by that of God, who prepares souls to receive his message. "See, I am sending you out like sheep into the midst of wolves: so be wise as serpents, and innocent as doves" (10:16). This is the diplomatic line adopted by honest, forthright apostles.

A magnificent hour of adoration last night. For the first time I managed to follow Mass in ideal fashion during adoration. Good results.

17 January
Peter's act of faith: "Lord, to whom can we go? You have the words of eternal life!" (John 6:68).

The relationship between nature and the supernatural helps us to understand that between humanity and God.

19 January
Recommending all one's concerns to God must effectively be a daily "struggle": a struggle in that all that one asks has to be submitted to his light and his will. It must be an echo of Israel's fight with the angel, a continuation of the unceasing biblical debate.

This year must be one of intensely hard work. A general revision of my life, an internal transformation, assiduous prayer, a study of French and English and perhaps a little work on possible future publications.

I must concoct a personal picture of Christianity, using passages from the Scriptures.

I believe the fundamental key to making progress in one's spiritual life is to eliminate complications and problems.

20 January
One of the problems that has particularly vexed me in my spiritual life is how, in what way and to what extent is there divine intervention in human affairs, especially in connection with a life of sanctification. Yesterday I suddenly saw a comparison between such intervention and the part played by nature in farming, and I drew some useful conclusions from it. Let us imagine a fertile and well-run farm. Neglect by the owner turns it into a desert. Now, one may ask: is it up to nature or man to restore the farm to its original beauty? In this case, the part that falls to man is immediately obvious. Man must work, sweat, plough, scythe, and so on. Without his toil the mechanism decreed by God's will for that farm is not set in motion. Man's contribution is indispensible and thus is willed by God.

Naturally, man will achieve better results the more he collaborates with the forces of nature, but his *intervention* is essential, so let's have no quietism. However, despite man's work and effort, a large part is left to the mysterious action of natural forces, so he may have an excellent year when he has done less work, and a disastrous harvest when he has worked really hard. In other words, a lot is owing to the action of nature, and this must be borne in mind.

As regards the *man-God relationship*, the same comparison is applicable, since everything is a copy, an image, an example. Nature too is a copy, a reflection of the supernal. To begin with, God requires man to toil, and this toil is his will. Since he created man free, he knows this toil is a true expression of man's faith. Man raises himself up to do God's will, as in his prayers he asks that God's will be done. Truly, this goes to show that man is "a little lower than the angels" (Psalm 8:5). His will has something divine about it. However, just as the farmer's toil is not arbitrary but obeys the laws of nature, by the same token the soul's toil to achieve its own sanctification has to obey the laws of sanctification. To discover and obey these laws is to ensure good results and fruitfulness. To sow at the right time, fertilize wisely and understand the seasons guarantees results, just as spiritual labour, humility, prayer, grace and sacrifice lead to spiritual fruitfulness.

Therefore one must toil, but in a given direction, along clearly defined lines.

And what are the laws to obey so that man's toil may bear fruit? The laws of the Gospel – Jesus' teaching and the true inspiration of the Holy Spirit. And to start with, the commandments are the first expression of the laws we have to discover, the culmination of natural law and the voice of conscience put in each of us by the Creator. As well as the commandments, the law which regulates everything is love: "Love and do what you wish" really is the best way to behave. *That which is dictated by love* becomes law, and it is man's duty to practise it. The evangelical text is extremely clear on this point: "For to all those who have more will be given, and they will have an abundance; but from those who have nothing, even what they have will be taken away" (Matthew 25:29).

It is a question, then, of committing acts of love, which thus become a habit. So a state of love is gradually achieved, which is, after all, a life of sanctity in that grace acts on our toil and conforms us to the image of Jesus, as Paul said: "For those whom he foreknew he also predestined to be conformed to the likeness of his Son" (Romans 8:29).

21 January

I shall have to meditate a bit on the meaning of the Gospel term, "The Kingdom of God". This evening during adoration some splendid thoughts occurred to me on the subject, which I must carefully sort out.

The Kingdom of God is the expression Jesus uses to describe the human-divine reality in which men will find themselves after the consummation of redemption and the coming of the Holy Spirit on earth. It is the life of the Mystical Body of Christ, the vital force of the Church, the reality of Christianity in its entirety. Members of tribes, nations, earthly kingdoms, republics and so on, though continuing to belong to these social groups as men, are introduced by baptism to a new human-divine reality called *the Kingdom of God*.

It is truly the Kingdom that Jesus mentioned to Pilate when he was being questioned: "My kingdom is not from this world" (John 18:36), even though elsewhere he had said, "the kingdom of God is among you" (Luke 17:21). Therefore it is not a Kingdom which is part of this world, and it does not have geographical boundaries. It is intangible and invisible to the eyes of the flesh, but it exists on earth as well; in men's souls, to be precise. It has its triumphs and is no stranger to defeat, expansion or contraction: in short, it is a Kingdom.

Naturally, the King of this Kingdom is God, and its capital lies in that *hidden* place we call "Heaven". Its citizens are the blessed, the angels, the souls in purgatory and, here on earth, the Christians. Of course, the most turbulent part of the Kingdom is on earth, but this is also the part where its most magnificent triumphs are achieved and where the most wonderful pages of its history are written.

These are the laws governing the earthly domains of the Kingdom (Matthew 5:3-10):

Blessed are the poor in spirit
Blessed are those who mourn
Blessed are the meek
Blessed are those who hunger and thirst for righteousness
Blessed are the merciful
Blessed are the pure in heart
Blessed are the peacemakers
Blessed are those who are persecuted for righteousness' sake

The *Kingdom* is promised to them: possession of the earth, consolation, repletion, mercy, a vision of God and being called the children of God. These things are the ultimate reward.

Jesus described some aspects of this Kingdom in his parables:

"The *Kingdom of heaven* may be compared to a king who gave a wedding banquet for his son" (Matthew 22:2).

This parable is fundamental because it is the mystical account of God's marriage to man in the person of Mary. Divine nature is united with human nature, and "the true mystery hidden throughout the centuries", the most sublime in all Christianity, comes to pass.

Man becomes a citizen of the Kingdom in a way which has no equal in any other sphere of human existence: he participates in the nature of God: "I say, you are gods" (Psalm 82:6). On entering the Kingdom man is deified, so from that moment he belongs to God's own family and is Christ's relative. And again:

"*The kingdom of heaven* may be compared to someone who sowed good seed in his field: but while everybody was asleep . . ." (Matthew 13:24-25).

"*The kingdom of heaven* is like a mustard seed, that someone took, and sowed in his field" (4:30-32; 13:31).

"*The kingdom of heaven* is like yeast that a woman took and mixed in with three measures of flour" (13:33).

"*The kingdom of heaven* is like treasure hidden in a field" (13:44).

"*The kingdom of heaven* is like a merchant in search of fine pearls; on finding one pearl of great value, he went and sold all that he had, and bought it" (13:45-46).

"*The kingdom of heaven* is like a net that was thrown into the sea and caught fish of every kind; when it was full, they drew it ashore, sat down, and put the good into baskets but threw out the bad" (13:47-48).

"*The kingdom of heaven* will be like this. Ten bridesmaids took their lamps, and went to meet the bridegroom . . ." (25:1 et seq.). *For the Lord* shall act like "a man [who], going on a journey, summoned his slaves and entrusted his property to them; to one he gave five talents, to another two, to another one . . . For to all those who have, more will be given, and they will have an abundance: but from those who have nothing, even what they have will be taken away" (25:14 et seq).

Sowing, fertility, the struggle between good and evil, silent growth, leavening, the joy of finding treasure, the appreciation of supreme values and beauty, the catch in the divine net, the final judgement, an invitation to be vigilant, to seek out, to make proper use of the gifts received – these are all points of reference for those elected to share the divine adventure of the Gospel. Note how the images of yeast, the net and seed all evoke silence and avoid all noise and confusion. The image of hidden treasure also evokes the silence of the one who finds it – the merchant harbours the joy of his great find in his heart. And what about the man who entrusts his concerns to others? In short, everything happens as it does in nature without anyone realizing it.

Jesus put the search for this Kingdom before all things, thus establishing a new scale of values for the free man: ". . . strive for his kingdom, and these things will be given to you as well" (Luke 12:31). He promised possession of it to those who seek it by deeds, not words: "Not everyone who says to me, 'Lord, Lord,' will enter the kingdom of heaven, but only the one who does the will of my Father" (Matthew 7:21).

Finally, he revealed that the way to achieve this is diametrically opposed to any human way: "Truly I tell you, unless you change and become like children, you will never enter the kingdom of heaven" (Matthew 18:3). And he left it open to people of all ages: "For the kingdom of heaven is like a landowner who went out early in the morning to hire labourers for his vineyard . . ." (Matthew 20:1 et seq.).

And what about Jesus' desire to establish this Kingdom? It was such an imperative that he included it in the prayer he himself composed: "Thy Kingdom come".

22 January

This evening during the hour of adoration I had the feeling that a very important act of faith was taking shape inside me. I was thinking of the Last Supper and repeated the words of Jesus, "Take; this is my body . . . This is my blood" (Mark 14:22-25). For Jesus, the wish and the deed are the same thing because he does not delude himself. The wish for, and the acceptance of, his sacrifice are the sacrifice itself. I tried to imagine what my feelings would be if I were faced with the proposition, "This is your body – offer it. This is your blood – are you ready to give it?" I perceived the extent of my immaturity and the infinite distance which separates my soul from a true acceptance of the sacrifice. So I said: "Father, imprint the image of your Son Jesus in my being – instil in me the same feelings, the same desires, the same obedience." And I seemed to hear him answer: ". . . but you must let yourself be moulded; let me create my firstborn Son, Jesus, in you . . . ."

I agreed. But I added immediately: "Don't abandon me. You know how little I am, how I feel and how helpless I am. Carry me. Above all, never leave me alone. You know how frightened I am when you don't keep in touch with me!"

An immense feeling of peace was the reply.

Milad said some impressive things in commenting on Peter's confession. Illuminated by the Father, Peter claims that Jesus is the Christ, and straight away he feels able to talk about the whole mystery. But he is wrong: understanding a thing doesn't necessarily mean total understanding. Milad ended by saying: "Life is a journey, and our discoveries are made a bit at a time, and our faith develops a bit at a time. What counts is to stay humble and very close to Jesus."

The majesty of God: titles invoking adoration

Him who is and who was and who is to come (Revelation 1:4).

The faithful witness (1:5).

The firstborn of the dead (1:5).

The ruler of the kings of the earth (1:5).

I am the Alpha and the Omega (1:8;22:13).

I am the beginning and the end (22:13).

I am . . . the Almighty (1:8).

I am . . . the first and the last (1:17;22:13).

I am the living one (1:18).

I have the keys of Death and of Hades (1:18).

Him who has the sharp two-edged sword (2:12).

The Son of God, who has eyes like a flame of fire, and whose feet are like burnished bronze (2:18).

Him who has the seven spirits of God (3:1).

The holy one, the true one (3:7).

Who opens, and no one will shut, who shuts, and no one opens (3:7).

The origin of God's creation (3:14).

The Amen (3:14).

The Lion of the tribe of Judah (5:5).

The Word of God (19:13).

The Lamb that was slaughtered (5:12).

Lord of lords and King of kings (17:14).

I am the root and the descendant of David (22:16).

The bright morning star (22:16).

In the beginning was the Word (John 1:1).

All things came into being through him (1:3).

In him was life (1:4).

The Word became flesh (1:14).

No one has ever seen God (1:18).

The Lamb of God, who takes away the sin of the world (1:29).

I am the bread of life (6:35).

Whoever believes in the Son has eternal life (3:36).

I am the good shepherd (10:11).

I am the gate (10:7).

I am the resurrection and the life (11:25).

I am the way, and the truth, and the life (14:6).

Glory to God in the highest heaven (Luke 2:14).

Hallowed be your name (11:2).

What do you have that you did not receive? (1 Corinthians 4:7).

The rock was Christ (10:4).

Blessed be the God and Father of our Lord Jesus Christ
  (2 Corinthians 1:3).

He has made him the head over all things for the church
  (Ephesians 1:22).

The corner-stone (2:20).

The boundless riches of Christ (3:8).

Though he [Christ] was in the form of God, he did not regard
  equality with God as something to be exploited, but emptied
  himself, taking the form of a slave (Philippians 2:6-7).

So that at the name of Jesus every knee should bend in heaven
  and on earth and under the earth, and every tongue should
  confess that Jesus Christ is Lord, to the glory of God the
  Father (2:10-11).

It is God who is at work in you, enabling you both to will and
  to work (2:13).

He is the image of the invisible God, the firstborn of all
  creation; for in himn all things in heaven and on earth were
  created, things visible and invisible (Colossians 1:15).

Through him God was pleased to reconcile to himself all things
  whether on earth or in heaven, by making peace through the
  blood of his cross (1:20).

How great among the Gentiles are the riches of the glory of this
  mystery, which is Christ in you, the hope of glory (1:27).

The God of peace (1 Thessalonians 5:23).

To Christ Jesus our Lord, who has strengthened me
  (1 Timothy 1:12).

To the King of the ages, immortal, invisible, the only God, be
  honour and glory forever and ever (1:17).
Christ, who gave himself a ransom for all (2:6).
For everything created by God is good (4:4).
High priest (Hebrews 9:11).
It is a fearful thing to fall into the hands of the living God
  (10:31).
Glorify the God and Father of our Lord Jesus Christ
  (Romans 15:6).

I am who I am (Exodus 3:14).
I am the Lord your God (20:2).
You shall not make wrongful use of the name of the Lord your
  God (20:7).
Where were you when I laid the foundation of the earth? . . .
  Who determined its measurements? Surely you know!
  Or who stretched the line upon it? On what were its bases
  sunk or who laid its corner-stone? (Job 38:4-6)

25 January

It is useless to pick out texts and neglect one's commitments. An
exercise of will is far more worthwhile. While talking to Milad
yesterday, I let myself be caught in the snare of vanity again. My
preoccupation with myself destroys sincerity and freedom in
communication and leaves me dissatisfied. This must be the last time!
I have to win free of greed too. Once a programme has been decided
upon I must stick to it.

The high spot of the day was the commentary on this Gospel text:
"If any want to become my followers, let them deny themselves, and
take up their cross and follow me" (Matthew 16:24). *A follower must
see himself as one condemned to death* (in those days the cross was a form
of torture reserved for slaves). Indeed, the following lines echo this
brutality: "For those who want to save their life will lose it, and those
who lose their life for my sake will find it" (16:25). And it concludes.
"For what will it profit them if they gain the whole world but forfeit

their life?" (16:26). This really is one of the harshest teachings of the Blessed Master, and it follows his first announcement of the Passion. A fitting conclusion!

26 January

In man's congenital, avowed, obvious, terrifying inability to achieve fulfilment, there is but one path to salvation: God.

God is our fulfilment.

God fulfils us through Christ. Just as in human existence and on a primordial level the father fulfils his child, the friend his friend, the bridgegroom his bride, in supernal life the Father fulfils his Son, Jesus fulfils his brother and the Holy Spirit fulfils his bride, the soul. This is a great comfort and I was consoled by it this morning during Communion thanksgiving.

God is my fulfilment.

29 January

Love, love, love – love God above all else, love one's neighbour, think of God with love, bear pain with love, act with love, live by love: this is Heaven's way to fulfil oneself and find God more easily.

It is pointless to waste effort on hypothetical prayers for concentration, and endless discussions which leave one sterile and empty, especially when there is time to spare, as now in the novitiate. These things are as good as useless.

Yesterday evening too, Milad shed valuable light on this concept: "Whoever wishes to be great among you must be your servant" (Matthew 20:26-27).

We can and we must have a supreme goal, and Jesus shows us the way: "Do you want to be the greatest? Put yourself last, and the more you serve others the greater you will be." That is the hierarchy of the Kingdom of God, and there lies the incentive to usher everyone else into what are truly the first places.

30 January

Last night Milad said some very profound things on the subject of this Gospel text about tolerance: "Whoever is not against us is for us" (Mark 9:40).

"*Whoever welcomes a righteous person in the name of a righteous person will receive the reward of the righteous*" (Matthew 10:41).

There really is an invisible Kingdom of Heaven the borders of which we cannot perceive and the inhabitants of which only God knows. Those people who have not yet entered the *visible* Kingdom of God belong to the invisible one. Jesus alone knows and sees all. How comforting this thought is! And how it illuminates our vocation as Little Brothers! How many people in the world can say, "For truly I tell you, whoever gives you a cup of water to drink because you bear the name of Christ will by no means lose the reward" (Mark 9:41).

31 January

One feature of our rule is the adoration of the Holy Sacrament. This adoration is a loving quest for the presence of Jesus in his human-divine existence and not only a spiritual quest for God. This almost tangible presence in the Eucharistic mystery ought especially to accustom us to detect the presence of Jesus and to channel our prayers in that direction. It is a consummation within the Church of a *truth* as yet too little reflected upon or comprehended: "God is among us."

One of the things I must try hardest to gain during my novitiate is personal knowledge of Jesus, as much by Eucharistic adoration as by meditation on the Gospel.

If it is true, however, that the depth of one's knowledge of Jesus depends on the depth of one's love for him, it is easy to understand the full extent of the involvement called for by the enterprise. And if it is also true that love is tested and witnessed to by pain, it is easy for me to grasp all the implications of this involvement.

FEBRUARY 1955

4 February
Mario¹ became a novice on 2 February, and so he is the third Italian to join the Little Brothers. Yesterday we went on a trip into the desert to celebrate. I went to the Col of Géryville.² Meanwhile the post is not getting through and I haven't had any letters for ten days.

5 February
Yesterday evening the mail arrived. Nothing important. This morning I got up fired with the idea of dedicating the day to being decisive and to acquiring the strength of spiritual energy. I need to sacrifice myself more. I must accustom myself to living in harmony with the Lord's Passion. I must try not to dissipate myself: I must try to accept and seek out the things that will prepare me for sacrifice, minute by minute.

Mary, help me!

Septuagesima Sunday
A number of circumstances have led me today to place "the stripping of myself" at the heart of my spiritual life. I cannot help but see God's merciful hand in all this intense activity.

During adoration over the past few days I had already heard the call to the cross. This morning Milad set the seal on it by overturning certain of my views, while placing *"the stripping of self for the love of Christ"* at the heart of every other religious action. By accepting this, and setting all the rest to revolve around it, I will finally be able to achieve the equilibrium I have unsuccessfully sought for so long.

The liturgy, the voice of the Lord, this place, the school I have enrolled in – everything must participate in this struggle of mine. Mary of Sorrows, intercede for me at the throne of the Lamb.

8 February

Yesterday I baked bread. Suddenly on Sunday evening Popol[3] informed me that I was to leave my old duties and dedicate myself to *la boulangerie*.[4] I spent the day with Brother Arturo. But my new job didn't last very long. Yesterday evening I was told that Milad preferred me among the olive trees. So I am going back to the sacristy and the garden. I was pleased with my new duties yesterday and today I am pleased with the old. That's how it should be. However, it was a good day, full of compensations. But perhaps I am wrong to think back on it and write about it, because Milad would tell me that none of this counts. A thing only counts if it springs from a total stripping of self. But I am so young in the spiritual life! God help me.

9 February

How fragile my confidence and my peace are! It takes the merest trifle to upset or destroy them, which is why it is far better to concentrate exclusively on stripping oneself of everything. Meanwhile, if one lets oneself be soothed by consolations, even spiritual ones, true peace will never be achieved, for it will be threatened even by a breath of wind.

The Eucharist

Upon the world is the memorial of the Lord's death: the Eucharist. The peace-bearing Host, the living and sacrificial presence of Christ, is the eternal perpetuation of the sacrifice on Calvary. The Mass continues the sacrifice of the High Priest, the adoration of the Lamb – he who is the Bridge to the world, the living Gate, the worshipper of the Father, the supreme Example; the Mass is the liturgical prostration of the creature before its Creator. It is and always will be the most important thing in the world, and it is strange how many Christians have not found this out.

Our religion ought to revolve around this mystery which, after all, is the sum of the two principal mysteries of our faith: the Oneness and Trinity of God and the Incarnation and Passion of Jesus. By contemplating and worshipping the Eucharist we have before us the whole, living, human-divine reality of the world. The Trinity is present, the Incarnation is visible, the Passion of the Lord is told, the Love of God is palpable.

It is all there in the Host: Jesus with his humanity, his prayer and his sacrifice; the Father contemplates his Son, consecrated for love of him; and the Holy Spirit, the Virgin and the angels are there too.

It is Paradise on earth, and our tremendous insensitivity and lack of faith show to what extent Jesus has been abandoned. Was it or was it not the express desire of men to have God with them? We asked for him, and what was the end result . . .?

"O Lord, give us faith."

The Jews had the Ark and in it they stored – strange coincidence – *the tablets and the manna*, truth and life, already foretold back then.

Solomon built the Temple and God granted his presence in the Holy of Holies, in the thick darkness of faith (cf. 1 Kings 8:12) – a divine preparation for the great mystery that was to become the heart of Christianity: the Eucharist.

The tablets of the Covenant? Too little: we shall have the author of the Covenant. Manna? Too little: we shall have the God-Man for food. We shall still have the darkness of faith like the darkness in the Temple, but this is only natural in the face of a religious dilemma based upon human testimony from which not even the Madonna was exempt: *Deus absconditus*. But there is one thing still to be said: the Eucharist – like creation, like mankind, like all things – was made not only for man but "to the glory of God". These two aspects are always present – the glory of God and the redemption of mankind. He who only perceives the latter would deprive himself of the true "compassion" of Christ. God first, humanity second.

Creation? *Per Ipsum factum est*,[5] and then for mankind.

The Incarnation? Yes, for man *propter nostram salutem* ('for our salvation'), but first to the glory of the Father. Jesus would have come – as the priest of humanity – even without the Fall. He is the worshipper of the Father, he represents all creation before the Father in his majesty.

And the Eucharist? A good deal of this mystery is owing to the

Father, over and above, of course, the sacrificial element which leads to redemption and which is the result of the existence of sin.

The Eucharist is the perpetuation of the Incarnation of Jesus, and the continuation of the perfect prayer which he addressed to the Father during the nights he spent on earth.

What is Jesus doing in the Eucharist? We might reply: "Waiting for mankind," and that is true, but principally "He is doing what he did on earth in his Incarnation."

O the infinite worth of his adoration! O the immensity of his hidden presence! O sublime hymn of love springing from his vital prostration before the Father! O sacerdotal, constant, valid offering of all which is of mankind, made by God become Man! O centre of *the created universe*, present in the humanity of Christ! O voice representing all the voices in the world! O holy prayer of all prayers!

Christ worships the Father in the Eucharist.

And as the expiator of sin? The Eucharist is the Sacrifice – it is the Lamb, the Slaughtered One – it is the remembrance of the Lord's death – it is the sum of all pain, all tears and all obedience. It is the *Peacemaker*. Justice and peace are met in Christ.

What suffering, what brutality, what a lack of faith is needed for one to abandon the Eucharist, not think of the Eucharist, not live according to the Eucharist. This is the greatest failing of Christianity today – or at least, of Christians. This is the point to concentrate on tomorrow. Countries in ignorance of the Eucharistic mystery, cities in evolution where Jesus is undiscovered by faith, acts of apostolacy made without him, prayers without him to interpret them, suffering without the possibility of offering it up. What does all our striving matter if it is not presented to the Father by him? What are our words worth if his voice is not joined with ours, or our prayers, without that symbol of *living Prayer*?

Grant me profound faith in the Eucharist!

12 February

There was Moses and the Law, and there was Elijah and the Prophecy. This linking of God's revelation to the two major figures in the Old

Testament is interesting. Moses had his revelation of God in the majesty
and power of a storm. Elijah had his in the mildness of a gentle breeze.
The former had to teach strength and respect, the latter gentleness
and mercy. Mount Oreb was witness to both pacts.

17 February
Yesterday during adoration I had an inspiration, which was always
to accept the path of abasement, concealment and humility, to ignore
insults and to overcome evil through good. In short, to have "the
same mind . . . that was in Christ Jesus" (Philippians 2:5). Meanwhile
I have given my gold watch to Milad.

18 February
There are three stages of mortification: the first is that of liberation,
and it anticipates the Gospel. It is John's penitence, and it is also
mentioned by Jesus: "Unless you repent, you will all perish" (Luke
13:3). The second belongs to the beatitudes and is filled with love and
peace. The third is the understanding of, and sharing in, the redemptive
suffering of Jesus. This third stage perfects life and is always the gift
of the Lord. To sum up:

"Repent, for the kingdom of heaven has come near" (Matthew 4:17).

"Blessed are the poor in spirit, for theirs . . ."(5:3).

"Blessed are you when people revile you and persecute you . . .
on my account" (5:11).

21 February
The Khaloua[6] should have started yesterday, but it was delayed by the
late arrival of the camels. Now we are all waiting. Last night Milad
talked about suffering, and as usual spoke very well. He commented
on Jesus' announcements of his death – announcements which were
not understood by those close to him then . . . nor by Christians later.
Suffering is a mystery we have to accept if we want to understand
anything at all about Christ. Many try to avoid it, but fruitlessly. It
is certain that the key to the mystery of suffering, and to so many
other mysteries, lies in love, but love too is a *mystery*.

25 February

The novitiate is deserted. Thirty-five of our number are on their way to Béni Abbès[7] and won't be back until about the end of March. I was with them until the dawn of the second day and slept with them in the tent, but I am now back[8] at El-Abiodh. I intend to put this month of greater solitude to good use. God help me!

On my way back yesterday I thought of that place in the front ranks to which we are naturally attracted, and the answer came to me very clearly: "It is among the lowliest of those who serve" (cf. Mark 10:43). Jesus said it, and he cannot be wrong. Lord, help me to achieve it.

First Sunday of Lent

The moment has come to do something a bit more demanding. My state of health, my commitment to the novitiate, the fact that time is now running out, all urge me to apply myself more seriously to my life.

First of all, having had a few problems in my relationships with my brothers lately, I must din some of Jesus' teachings into my head.

Evil is defeated by good. When dislike washes over you, when you are sorely tried, when you are the victim of injustice, your path is clearly signposted: follow Jesus. Never, ever let yourself get a persecution complex (something you are all too familiar with, having suffered from one at the hands of you know who). *Be generous and big, rise above minor irritations*, which are fatal in a close community. You must also take advantage of Lent to concentrate on penitence. There will be no lack of opportunity, especially where food is concerned.

Having got that out of the way, now for the most important thing. Any rule, even the most rigorous, can become a totally futile thing if it is not applied with love in its purest sense. Exactly the same is true for poverty. When you have stripped yourself of everything you still find yourself clinging to some rag, a needle, a blanket, and you are more miserly and grudging than before. Resisting a spirit of avarice and selfishness and the temptation to hoard is terrible, because we are dealing with our own nature, which is utterly corrupt. I must put all my strength into it, especially in little things, and perhaps I ought to relinquish my so-called *tidiness*, where selfishness frequently lurks. Before, I was fond of a pair of trousers I brought from Rome. By chance I put on another pair, and now I am attached to those. I take even things like a spool of thread, some insulating tape, a pair of scissors and there I am – attached, fond, enslaved. Freeing oneself from everything, accepting only what you are given, not holding on to anything, especially the things you are fond of, must be a daily exercise. With my ability to adapt, I am even attached to this place.

Lord, help me, inspire me, correct me: I want to succeed. Heaven forfend that I should come here and fail to learn these lessons! So, to summarize: (1) *Don't keep anything* as a personal possession; (2) *Don't take anything*, especially in the kitchen, given your assigned duties there and your craftiness.

28 February

16.15 – 17.15. An hour of adoration. Perhaps for the first time I strove side by side with God. How sweet is the Lord! "*Have faith*," he told me. "Be faithful. *Seek and you shall find me!* Simplicity and love is the path you must take. Refuse the rest. Don't let self-absorption, egocentricity or feelings of persecution creep up on you." Then he told me: "I want to become one with you" – I was taking Communion at evening Mass at the time. "My God, I love you, I love you," I replied. During the reading of the Epistle I meditated on the story of Joseph, who was sold by his brothers (Genesis 37 et seq.).

MARCH 1955

2 March

During Holy Mass I had a flash of inspiration which I must jot down. Why are personal relationships so difficult, even in small things? Why is there so much antipathy, spirit of persecution, sadness and so on? Because, unlike Jesus, *we have not chosen to come last*. This fundamental error causes so much confusion and unhappiness.

I pressed the Lord – for I have realized that my prayers need to be more forceful and insistent – to grant me this grace, which is, after all, the spirit of Jesus [cf. Philippians 2:6].

How disgraceful of me to insist on my rights when Jesus did not – he stayed silent and let himself be beaten! He certainly had the right to shout, to hit out, to make claims! Yet what about me? How right Milad was when he said the the most direct route is to "strip the self"! What a powerful Christian truth this is!

Another thought for today: I must do everything in God's sight and not my own. Agreed? That way I won't do too many stupid things!

Why does the Church evolve so slowly? Does it depend on God being reluctant to give himself, or on mankind? Certainly, the development of the Church was entrusted to men, and they run it. But why the slowness, the delays, the problems? There is but one reason: they don't work *with him*; they work alone, and the results are in proportion to their small-mindedness. It is the case of the flex and the electric current all over again. There are flexes, and a lot of them! But where's the current? What a mess!

God really has placed himself in human hands, and humanity does not make use of him or seek him out. That is why there are so many personal and collective failures.

4 March

As of today I am dead to my own plans and am adopting the plans of Jesus. What I do from now on I shall do for love of him, after having first sought him out in prayer. I feel I have changed my whole outlook. Anyway, what point would there be in gaining the world and displeasing Jesus? Why this pointless struggle? And for whom? For what? What self-deception on the part of Christians – and apostles! I want Jesus' love as well as all the rest. I want to place him before me, not walk in front of him! Lord, forgive the pride which has almost always led me to walk ahead of you, thinking I was doing the right thing. And what did I achieve? Mistakes, mistakes, mistakes! Useless things, vain plans: empty posturings.

Forgive me, Jesus. Impress these thoughts in my soul so that they may become a reality. *I never want to change from this frame of mind again.*

Let's have a look at the Bible to confirm this divine truth.

Abraham? His election – his destiny – the test – the promise – his vocation: who arranged it for him?

Joseph? Egypt – the famine – God's people making their home in a distant land.

Moses? The Hero of the world – his preparation – the promised land – manna, water from the rock: who was responsible?

Who orchestrates the yearning for Christ which runs throughout the Old Testament? Man or God? "Go," says the Lord. "Find." "Speak." "Tell." But to do that all the time and try to change the order of things would be to falsify the outcome of our religious history. Mary? Is she the leader or is she the "servant" of the Lord? Is it she who plans for God or does God guide her? Joseph? God says: "Go." "Come back." "Do . . ."

It is always the same story.

God's plan

All creation is God's, *Factorem coeli et terrae.*[1] Mankind? God said to Job: "Tell me . . . Who determined its measurements . . . or who stretched the line upon it?" (Job 38:4-5).

However, God wanted to give man a place in his creation and in a way intended him to help nature with his work. Man completes the work of creation by his toil, and one cannot help but notice the difference between a vineyard and a stretch of scrub.

Redemption is entirely God's: its conception, its preparation and its accomplishment. Down there at the bottom of the abyss man could not even begin to imagine such a concept. In this case too, it is God's will that man take part in his work of redemption, to such an extent that we can do the same work: we are invited to save souls, which means helping them to share in redemption.

And there is the mystery of the Church. Whose is the initiative, whose the plan? What are the ways, the methods? Let's take an example: Once there was a garden in the desert – man before the Fall. The passing of centuries, neglect and invasions destroyed it. Now it has become a part of the desert – sin. How does God's plan work through man – through the Church?

He who goes out, wields a hoe and toils is certainly man. Without that work the original garden cannot be restored. But what is the difference? It is that today God has made water flow in the subsoil once more. Man's task is to bring it up to the surface and dig irrigation channels, hoe, sow seeds and plant.

But is man free to follow his own devices? No, because his plan *must* be subjected to the laws which govern him as well as the garden: the seasons, the quality of the seed, water, the sun and so forth. This is man's mistake: he ignores those laws and works independently of them. He makes irrigation channels on the surface, not where the water is to be found – this is activism. He works and sweats, without taking the realities which constrain him into account.

Those are the mistakes I have committed a hundredfold! I work on the surface, make my own plans and . . . I don't make use of the water or watch out for the sun. In the desert – and the world is a terrifying desert – water is essential for a garden. It is the *sine qua non*. Indeed Jesus said: *Sine me nihil potestis facere* (John 15:5).

And as for preparation of the plan, is it not far fairer, more beneficial, more humble, truer and more worthwhile to turn to someone who knew the garden as it was before, because he made it and worked in it for a very long time and is the true gardener? What's more, he bought it back with his blood.

This is where lack of faith comes in: not taking any notice of him – not hearing him – not seeing him – not respecting or seeking him.

God, my God, forgive my faithless past! Grant me plenty of faith in future. *Faith, faith, faith*: means to see God filling all the world.

6 March

After compline in the chapel this evening I understood for the first time that "leaving the initiative to God" also affects prayer, and possibly that more than anything. Be quiet a moment – come into his presence – learn to listen. Got that? Above all, change your attitude. Learn to take and listen, and not only give and talk.

With regard to the temptation to be over-zealous in noting the faults and sins of others – one which has plagued me considerably recently – I open the life of St Teresa, and there it is (ch. XIII, para. 10). *A clear answer.*

10–18 March

A holiday in hospital in Mascara.[2] Things to remember: we think of pain as a disruption of our work or our prayer or our union with God. Thus we find it hard to bear. I must learn to think of it as work, prayer and union with God. Perhaps I shall learn to bear it more easily then. A delightful hour: I understood the meaning of Ecclesiastes for the first time. Let me close by saying that it is a magnificent book – a worthy twin to the book of Job, but in the opposite sense, of course.

19 March: St Joseph's Day

This year I have received *the special, extra special, superlative gift* of a great member of the Holy Family. Joseph was absolutely incredible. I believe he has irrevocably become a part of my life, and I of his. Over and above the role he may play in my vocation, which is to love the family of Nazareth, something personal has happened which I shall never forget. I have understood, as never before, what *belief in another person* means in faith.

APRIL 1955

2 April
This is my forty-fifth birthday. Gifts have been pouring in, and today put the finishing touch to the gift I received on the Feast of St Joseph. It has been a truly exceptional day, beginning with vespers yesterday evening.

I asked for the gift of living my faith continuously, without the perpetual ups and downs of a normal life, illuminated here and there by faith. Since faith alone would be worthless, the answer came to me that one must permanently live by love. A marvellous hour of adoration both last night and this afternoon.

3 April
The place chosen by Love is the lowliest of all. That is today's revelation. How profoundly I have realized this truth taught by Jesus who truly put himself last. I too must try for the last place, and when I have found it I shall have true peace.

Palm Sunday
What comfort today brings and how enthusiastically I waved the palm of my faith before Jesus!

I have the impression that my novitiate is moving into a constructive phase of faith and love. I spend infinitely sweet hours in a state of grace. God really is love! From now on I intend not to let a single instant go by without illuminating it with faith; not to do anything without the guidelines of faith; not to speak a word without examining it in the same light. I feel that in this way I have finally regained my integrity.

This morning Jesus told me that he loved me.

Monday of Holy Week

Learning to become bread and wine is what lies at the root of it all. Bread to give life, wine to give joy. Jesus became bread and wine and then he said: "This is my body, this is my blood." He gave himself to be eaten and he vouchsafed the infinite joy of love and salvation. I asked for the grace that, before I die, I may share Jesus' feelings and be able to say those same words, to show that I am offering myself up completely. Jesus promised that if I have faith, it will be granted.

This evening after adoration, I admired the flowers that have invaded the olive grove. They make a perfect image of fertility. I was reminded of the passage in the Scriptures which says, "I will look with favour upon you and make you fruitful and multiply you; and I will maintain my covenant with you" (Leviticus 26:9).

What a magnificent cry of love! Oh, if I only knew how to make proper use of the fruitfulness of my God and go to him with love and bear fruit in spirit, sanctity and soul! I would be able to raise the children of Abraham from stone! Even if I were as unyielding as stone, Jesus would be able to raise children from me (cf. Matthew 3:9).

Easter Day

In silence. I don't know why, but these past few days the Lord has been silent. It is certain he is displeased, but I can't think what the reason might be. However, it is fair: I cannot expect to know everything.

Low Sunday

The Easter aridity in my soul came to an end when a sudden thought occurred to me during Milad's lesson. Jesus *always* redeems. The Scriptures say: "To you all flesh shall come. When deeds of iniquity overwhelm us, you forgive our transgressions" (Psalm 65:2-3), and day after day Jesus relieves us of this burden. The Jews did not want to accept this divine generosity. They counted on the Law, they needed to feel that they could free themselves through good deeds. Moreover, it is not easy to accept a gift wholeheartedly without feeling the need to reciprocate: only love and spiritual childhood make us able to accept without wanting to give in return. *Only a child can do so, because it knows it has nothing and is nothing. It truly appreciates the gift without pointless agonizing.*

Lord, let me be a child before your immense gift.

23 April

During my happy moments of prayer the thought persists that *it is the Lord who directs things.* How proud we are if we irresponsibly overturn things, believing ourselves to be self-sufficient and sure guides, and how proud we are also if we are able to admit after a great struggle that things aren't like that after all. This is something I must achieve through acts of faith. I must reduce myself to the status of a bride. A bride does not lead, she is led. Her existence is ruled by the thought of the bridegroom. *It is all up to him.*

Even if this were not precisely the case, *how could God fail to reward such an attitude, as being the highest acknowledgement of his omnipotence, and the greatest possible manifestation of love on the part of his creature?*

I must therefore build on this by learning to accept that he will act, he will guide, he will call, he will indicate, he will make fruitful. He, only he. And I must be as childlike as possible, as biddable as possible, as helpless as possible.

27 April

The Patronage of St Joseph.

Hail Joseph, full of grace – the Lord is with you. Blessed are you among men, and blessed is Jesus, the son entrusted to you. St Joseph, custodian of God, pray for us sinners now and in the hour of our death. Amen.

If the first Joseph, the son of Jacob, suffered for his faith, how much more did the great Joseph suffer, chosen as he was by God for such a secret, profound, delicate, terrible mission? To preserve Mary's virginity, and to accept it in the light of a mystery of faith, reveals such great nobility on his part that the mere thought of it makes each of the faithful tremble.

28 April

I must live my life as a novice down to the smallest details, and I must derive the greatness of poverty, chastity and, above all, obedience, from these little things. St Joseph, help me.

30 April

St Catherine of Siena. This evening, during adoration, I made a resolution not to drink wine any more. I must also implement this great truth: "Unless your righteousness exceeds that of the scribes . . .' (Matthew 5:20).

Do you want a good plan to follow? Here it is: *Quae placita sunt semper.*[1] Try it.

MAY 1955

2 May
Adore self. Distort goodness. Believe oneself to be a guide.

Jesus replies: "Love the Lord and serve him alone. Unless your righteousness exceeds . . ." [cf. Matthew 5:20].

Sine me, nihil potestis (John 15:5).[1]

3 May
Having God for an ally could well be man's proudest boast, which is why such an alliance is achieved in the darkness of faith. The same thing goes for the possession of God's omnipotence. Only someone who will not use it for himself and who is completely detached from it may possess it. This is also true for glory. Only someone who is humble enough not to want it may have it.

5 May
This evening, during adoration, I had one of those lucid flashes of illumination which can only come from on high, about God's way of acting. The hidden God acts in a very similar way to Jesus in Nazareth. The Eucharist too is a silent Nazareth. Not only did Jesus live, and still lives, his hidden life, but so do the Father and the Spirit.

God's revelation does not come in the great wind but in the sheer silence heard by Elijah (cf. 1 Kings 19:12). He does that so as not to suffocate or oppress us and to respect our freedom.

How different to our mode of behaviour! What a commotion, what an uproar, what an intrusive presence is ours! That is what gives rise to inappropriate and off-putting clericalism, and it is also what causes temporalism, imperialism and Messianism.

7 May

Action is the expression of thought, and testifies to it. For God that is not the case, because his thought and his will to act coincide. "This is my body," Jesus says, and his Passion is accomplished. It is different for us, which is why we must think of action as the demonstration of faith. Only aspirations which are potential deeds have any value in the spiritual life. Otherwise, as the Lord says: "Not everyone who says to me, 'Lord, Lord' . . ." (Matthew 7:21).

Action. This is the point on which to examine one's conscience, especially for those, like me, who fall into the common trap of mistaking the wish and the thought for the deed; we rejoice in the mere wish and . . . move on. In the end one is back where one started, only sadder. "Between the thought and the deed . . ." says the Italian proverb, and that goes for the spiritual life too.

9 May

Martha and Mary (Luke 10:38 et seq.).

Martha worries, Mary chooses prayer. The simple but direct and true path she follows is: *listen to God talking about himself.* Too often prayer concentrates on the self, whereas the great thing is to forget oneself and think only of God.

15 May

Days pile on days and weeks on weeks, passing quickly as all seasons lived with intensity do. It is the first sign that things are well with nature and, even more so, with the supernatural.

The world of my past seems more distant and unappealing all the time, and only yesterday, as I was dreaming of some possible future destination, I beguiled myself with the picture of a lonely hermitage where I could serve God alone.

Your Kingdom come – The Kingdom of God is where *truth, goodness and beauty* are paramount. All that is good, harmonious and truthful is part of God's Kingdom.

Your will be done – God can only want goodness, and he wants it with all the intensity and power of his holiness. Indeed, what is holiness if not a desire for good?

> The pure in heart
> The peacemakers
> The merciful
> Those who thirst for righteousness
> The poor in spirit
> The innocent who are persecuted (cf. Matthew 5)

Who are they if not those who have chosen goodness, truth and beauty? They belong to the Kingdom.

The Ascension of the Lord

All our distractions, infidelities and insensitivity do not detract at all from the great truth which gives us so much hope: after his resurrection Jesus ascended into Heaven.

The most important thing for every creature is the Word Incarnate. Jesus, the Son of God, ascended to Heaven, taking his divinity and his humanity with him.

It is a completely new theme in God's story: the Son of Man is glorified. Even in us there is this basic need for glory, and he will grant it if we are faithful to his Son. Like him and like Mary, we too shall be glorified, reconciled, made new and resurrected.

What a wonderful gift! What a response to the needs of human nature, which was created by God with this tremendous destiny already mapped out for it!

Nazareth. What is God's lesson for us in the mystery of Nazareth? What are the facts of the matter? For thirty years the Word Incarnate led the most ordinary existence imaginable and did nothing to alter the course of events or modify any situation.

What does this mean? It means that every action in human life has the potential for absolute perfection. If God-made-man was able to demonstrate the absolute perfection of his spirituality in the course of his ordinary life, it means that every human action, even the most insignificant and humdrum, has the potential to be a perfect offering to God. This is very important for us, accustomed as we are to thinking that only exceptional events count. We take such pride in, and always opt for, the extraordinary things in life.

24 May

Any summary of our lives might well have this impressive title: *failure*, which is a very different thing from the one it ought to have: *poverty*. They both lead to the same thing in the end, but . . . what different attitudes! How much less bitterness there is in the latter!

That we are poor is a fact, but it is something else again to accept this poverty with joy (beatitude). It is quite another thing still to think of oneself as being rich and then to dicover one's poverty through the bitter experience of failure. That's how it has been for me, and right up until the present day, 24 May 1955, I have gone from failure to failure. Presumptiousness was what tripped me up, even when it was not intentional; especially when it was . . . *good, spiritual and apostolic*, in fact. Let's face the truth: I have always made my own plans. In my prayers I have always concentrated on doing, thinking and planning. *I have always felt that my future was firmly in my own hands.*

Now I have almost touched bottom. The earth is closed and hostile. Heaven is almost mute in answer to my futile prayers.

Yes, *I have indulged in futile prayer* – the sort which goes like this – always like this – "My will be done" – and which seeks to put God at my disposal (naturally to good ends!).

Now I am fed up – I declare my insolvency before Heaven and Earth. I want to be sent to prison for fraudulent bankruptcy, and when I am shut in the enforced silence of my richly deserved cell, I shall begin to meditate seriously on Charles de Foucauld's prayer, which I am giving here:

> *Father, I surrender myself to you.*
> *Do with me what you will.*
> *I thank you*

for everything you do with me:
I am willing to do anything,
I accept everything, on condition that
your will be done in me
and in all your creatures.
I want nothing else, my God.
I surrender myself to you
with total trust.
I put myself in your hands
without reservation, because you
are my father.

After which, I have only one thing to declare before signing the statement of my "insolvency". From now on I shall try my hardest not to set myself up in business, or see myself in the guise of an industrialist, a factory owner or an entrepreneur; instead I shall *go into service*. And to start with I shall ask St Joseph to take me on as apprentice in his workshop.

Who knows!

As for apostolic plans: *zero*. Spiritual plans even less: *zero* minus *zero*. When similar temptations sweep over me I must instantly unleash my faith: God will do it – God will provide – God will take care of it.

My part is to do his will.

Most Blessed Mary, whose feast-day this is[2] (Dolce and Em are surely somewhat responsible for all this), grant us your motherly smile. It will be our surest help!

27 May

Poverty means not needing things. In this sense God is truly poor because he needs nothing. He is everything.

It is normal to be conscious of one's own limitations in prayer. It must always be so, because our nature is defective. In drawing closer to God we draw closer to the source, the potential and the well-spring of everything. All we have to do is want it. This is the proper relationship to sustain with God. *Fons vincit sitientem.*[3]

Pentecost

There are two particular aspects of the apostolate to be noted: the first is "the frame of mind" of the apostle, or the spiritual attitude of a person who, having known Jesus, is spurred to bear witness and spread the word.

The second concerns the ways and means by which the apostolate is carried out, of which, as can be seen from the history of the Church, there is an infinite variety.

There is one other point to be made, and it concerns the *apostle*.

There is the official apostle, invested with authority (the powers that be), and there is the friend of Jesus, the individual Christan who, to be an apostle, must possess at least "the spirit" of one and follow the instructions of the powers that be.

If Jesus had always used the most humanly efficient means possible in his apostolate, there would be no more problems, and today the apostolate would concentrate simply on the technical aspects of spreading the word.

Instead it is apparent – and this is one mystery which will never be solved – that Jesus did not use rational methods, nor did he exploit the power of intelligence. There is something irrational in him, and it is a feature which runs through the whole history of the Church. The economics of redemption don't use decimals or the American monetary system. There is, and always will be, a kind of *folly* which only those close to Jesus can fully understand; an irrationality which is known as "the madness of the cross". To take it a step further – since true "irrationality" does not exist in a universe sustained by God, who is ultra-rational – what do people mean when they talk about this "irrational" element I have mentioned? Careful thought is needed to understand the problem.

"Irrationality" in the apostolate; is it not perhaps divine intervention which lies outside the scope of human influence, but which certainly has its own logic, laws and criteria? When saying that in his apostolate Jesus did not obey human logic, it cannot be claimed that he did not obey some other form of logic. He included the prime mover in his work: God the Father. This is the non-human element introduced by Jesus, and later by the blessed souls: God, who is anything but irrational, though he does not obey the canons of human reason. Jesus was not a scribe, nor a doctor; he was not rich or powerful (in human terms) because for him the problem was not so much the *rapid* spreading of the Gospel as secret fertilization, ploughing in depth and the mysterious watering with his blood.

From time to time the form of the apostolate may change, but one thing remains constant: the true protagonist is God, and ignoring him means to condemn oneself to failure.

The two elements, human and divine, are in proportion to one another, but since the part that we are tempted to leave out, or at least to forget, is the divine, things are always unbalanced on that side.

The image of creating an oasis in the desert is an apt one here. Water, the seasons, fertility . . . how many things pass unnoticed by the careless farmer who only considers his own involvement and his own work!

There is one last thing to be said. What, after all, is the apostolate? It leads to God. And how can something lead to God without God? And there we are, back at the great law governing all that is irrational – *love*. Love decides everything, explains everything and is the root and purpose of everything. *It is God.* Only God, and therefore only love; only love, and therefore only God. God obeys love and love carries all before it, because it is God himself.

30 May

Let us imagine that a blessed soul in Heaven is ordered by God to descend to earth and live out a whole human span. How would it spend this parenthesis between two eternities, this instant conceded to it by love? I think it would immediately try to imitate the life of Jesus, by loving and living for the Father. Then, affected by the sight of a world so different from the Kingdom of God, it would ask one thing only: "To atone, atone and atone." Jesus said, "Lord, you didn't want sacrifices or burnt offerings; you gave me a body, and I have come to do your will" (Hebrews 10:5-7). The blessed soul's will would be the same as Jesus' will was: "to atone through suffering and self-immolation".

This, then, is the highest goal for a Christian on earth – the most perfect possible imitation of the Master, the surest way, the most profound truth: to suffer, to die for love, to atone for the sins of the whole world, self-immolation for truth and justice; to put oneself last, to love, to be forgotten and not be taken into account; in other words, to live as Psalm 21 and Isaiah 53 suggest.

JUNE 1955

Trinity Sunday

I am half-way through my novitiate, and this feast-day is especially dear to my heart. I would like this to be the point of departure for a new phase in my spiritual life. Something has been resolved within me, there has been no lack of blessings and my direction has become far more clear. Let's try to take stock, then – but after I have made a confession, and have thus achieved a purer state of grace.

The enemy which blocks a greater revelation of Christ and the spread of the Holy Spirit in me is certainly pride. I saw this with greater clarity during the Col retreat.

Too often I do things for people and not for God, and all this ends by becoming the foe of freedom and of justice. Therefore I must do my best to amend the intention of my actions by always standing in God's sight. As regards *justice* I must accept the law of doing, taking, resting, eating and working, on a basis of equality for all.

Then, if I want to achieve justice through love, in the choices I make – which ought to be part of my vocation – all I have to do is choose to be last, in the closest imitation of Jesus.

Thoughts

Sin is the past, weakness and frailty are the present.

* Pride is to be found above all in intellect.
* Our adoration begins with Christ our mediator, teacher and interpreter and must have the Most Holy Trinity as its goal.
* Supreme piety is the adoration of the Trinity within us, and then one can even (in a certain sense) do without the sacraments.

* *Do you want to run faster?*
Choose to be last.
* *Do you want more freedom?*
Choose to be last.
* *Do you want to understand Jesus better?*
Choose to be last.
* *Do you want to love more?*
Choose to be last.
* *Do you want to serve justice?*
Choose to be last.
* *Do you want to be loved?*
Choose to be last.
* *Do you want greater joy?*
Choose to be last.
* *Do you want to teach by example?*
Choose to be last.
* *Do you want to understand the meaning of adoration?*
Choose to be last.
* *Do you want to achieve peace?*
Choose to be last.

Indeed, Jesus said: "The last will be first" (Mark 10.31). However, this must all be done for love and not for the sake of subtle pride.

Corpus Christi
God's love is boundless. He created, he renewed, he healed, he forgave and forgave again, he has always forgiven; he suffered, he let himself be killed, he became bread, he became almost nothing; he touched the bottom and there he found peace: in the heart of man.

I was thinking today that if God communicates himself to us, or in other words gives us his love, a similar pattern of descent will happen for us too; we too will tread the path of his Passion until we find peace in the total giving of self.

Jesus, grant me this gift. Burn away the impurities in my soul which prevent love from taking hold. Let me die for you and for yours, the human race, and start by giving me the desire for, the quest for, and pleasure in, being last: Jesus.

Texts on love

"For a brief moment I abandoned you, but with great compassion I will gather you . . . Just as I swore that the waters of Noah would never again go over the earth, so have I sworn that I will not be angry with you and will not rebuke you . . . O afflicted one, storm-tossed and not comforted!" (Isaiah 54:7-11).

"So I will become like a lion to them, like a leopard I will lurk beside the way. I will fall upon them like a bear robbed of her cubs . . . Shall I ransom them from the power of Sheol? Shall I redeem them from Death? O Death, where are your plagues? O Sheol, where is your destruction?" (Hosea 13:7 et seq.). "*I shall ransom them from the hands of Hell. I shall redeem them from Death. I shall be your death, O Death. I shall be your sting, O Hell.*"

"A hair out of place offends the beloved."

"To you all flesh shall come, when deeds of iniquity overwhelm us" (cf. Psalm 65:2-3).

The gift of wisdom at its purest allows us to "live God" for love's sake.

And since love demands equality, we shall love God with the same intensity with which he loves us. This, in fact, is Paradise.

Vespers of the Sacred Heart

We were exhorted to imitate Jesus in his life of sorrow. This was the main text:

C'est qu'il a poussé devant nous comme un rejeton, comme *une tige d'un sol aride*. Il n'avait ni aspect ni beauté pour que nous le contemplions, ni apparence pour que nous nous complaisions en Lui.

Il était méprisé et *le dernier des hommes, homme de douleurs et habitué à la maladie. Comme quelqu'un devant qui on se voile la face – méprisé, et nous n'avons fait de Lui aucun cas*[1] (Isaiah 53:2-3)

Sacred Heart of Jesus, as your feast-day gift grant that I may make this text part of my life. That is all I ask.

Is it not the plan of your own life, after all? Here are some very explicit references. Bethlehem, the Flight to Egypt and Nazareth are the first events in this plan.

"*He grew up . . . like a root out of dry ground*" (Isaiah 53:2), and nothing could be more arid than that: Jesus' roots even included Rahab, the prostitute of Jericho. "*He had no form or majesty that we should look at him.*" Who noticed Jesus during the thirty years he spent leading an ordinary existence?

But let's move on to the supreme moment of his humiliation on "the road to Calvary". Here he was "*despised and rejected by others, a man of suffering and acquainted with infirmity; and as one from whom others hide their faces he was despised, and we held him of no account . . . we accounted him stricken, struck down by God, and afflicted*" (Isaiah 53:3-4).

Then they spat in his face, and some punched him while others slapped him.

"We want Barabbas!"

When they had stripped him they dressed him in a purple robe. They wove a crown of thorns and put it on his head, and they placed a reed in his right hand. And then, kneeling before him, they mocked him (cf. John 19).

The Feast of St John the Baptist

As usual the great Baptist has come bearing gifts. This year it was an hour spent with the little family from Nazareth. Milad spoke about the Madonna with great force and originality. He brought her vividly to life with a realism which my ears and eyes are unused to, spoiled as they are by the Marian celebrations so common to Christianity, where the majesty almost completely eclipses the mother.

Let us examine one of her attributes.

Mary's greatness lies in loyalty to her faith. Her privileges as mother of the Saviour are a gift from God, not hers through merit. Where she does have merit, however, is in her assent, her steadfast loyalty to the holy demands made on her. First and foremost she is the product of the entire history of the Jewish religion and of her people, with all their hopes and dreams.

The Angel's greeting took her by surprise; she asked for explanations and illumination, in keeping with her adventurous and forthright nature. And then she said "Yes" – an event of tremendous importance for the whole course of history.

Mary never betrayed her faith, even when faced with the most terrible trials, and she rose to the occasion every time the Lord made demands on her.

Her honour was at stake with the one she loved most of all: Joseph. She waited, kept silent and obeyed. The second great test was certainly the flight into Egypt and the massacre of the innocents, the tragedy provoked by the birth of her son. What could her situation possibly have had in common with the splendid and sensational coming of the Messiah? An escape by night followed by exile and the massacre. And God? Where was God, the God of hosts?

Then there was the test God subjected Mary to, leaving her in the darkness of faith when Jesus got lost: "Did you not know . . .?" (Luke 2:49). "Mary treasured all these words and pondered them in her heart" (2:19). At each stage a fresh demand would be made on her, in line with God's plans for his creation. She reappeared in the life of her son at times of crisis, watching the tragedy of it with terrible grief, and sustained only by her faith. Then she travelled to Ephesus with John in the hope of joining her beloved son once more through death, and we have no further news of her.

St Peter's Day

God, my *Creator*! Source and root of my being, I love you. I seek you. You are everything to me.

Now that I am tainted by sin, re-create me, renew me, take me back to your creative embrace, and give me back the aspect you envisaged for me when you made me.

Life-giving air, water for those dying of thirst and bread for the hungry are as nothing, compared with what you are to me.

You are the arms in which I have my existence, the root on which

I stand, the Whole on which I depend. I am yours, make me yours; I am in you, gather me closer to you. Remember what your Spirit said in Zechariah: "made beautiful with my beauty" [9:17]. All the rest is mine, but unfortunately the only thing left is sin.

God, I love you.

JULY 1955

3 July

After a period of lassitude, the incentive to concentrate more on will-power has come back with full force. It's always the same old story, as I wriggle out of my commitments. Mary's example is decisive. There was divine intervention, awe-inspiring revelations and a foreordained plan, but . . . she travelled the road from Nazareth to Aïn Karim, and the angels certainly didn't carry her. Without doubt, it is a good thing to rely heavily on God and believe that only he acts, but collaboration as an act of love, in response to his call, is our inexorable duty.

The whole of Scripture testifies to this, logic demands it and the whole life of mankind demonstrates it.

I asked Mary to grant me the virtue of the mystery of the visitation, so that I might learn always to respond to the prompting of the Spirit by putting myself at the service of love.

The mystery of collaboration can be compared to the love between a bridegroom and his bride. The bridegroom summons but the bride has to say yes. Each birth is the fruit of this voluntary coexistence and collaboration. Though the relationship with God is infinitely more exalted – so much so that he is everything – despite this, and by his will, the response is mankind's to make. Without that response the miracle does not happen.

What if Abraham hadn't responded? What if Jacob hadn't wrestled with the angel? What if Moses had not set out? What if Mary had not agreed? It would have been the same because God, having created man almost godlike in his freedom, wanted it that way, and he never repents of his gifts.

So the question is this: God prompts the creature and gives it the outline of his will. *By faith* the creature understands what it must do.

The charity within the creature, sparked to life by the Holy Spirit which is love, agrees and acts.

God's holy work in the world stems from this action.

A life of holiness then, is nothing other than listening unceasingly for the voice and being ready to do his will.

6 July

"Never say: I was right. Do not defend yourself even when unjustly attacked. Do not talk about yourself. Do not speak ill of others. Do not seek to be loved" (St Teresa).

Accept death day by day. How wonderful it sounds – how hard it is to put it into practice!

And yet, it is the only way to find peace here on earth. Without that acceptance there is only the desolation of a drawing-room at dawn: the smell of things extinguished, mustiness, a feeling of emptiness, lack-lustre furnishings, filth that comes back to mind and kills any possible joy.

17 July

My reading of St John of the Cross has been particularly blessed by grace. It has been a real help to me this week. Here is a summary of his "Nothings":

> *To earthly goods*
> *To one's own opinion*
> *To one's own worth*
> *Even to graces received*
> *To oneself*

This road leads to the way of the cross and the crucifixion of the ego. You will be buried with Christ, which is a prelude to being resurrected with him for ever.

The spiritual life then, is a journey, so a guide is needed to reveal the Father to us during two fundamental moments in the life of mankind. "*This is my Son, the Beloved; listen to him!*" (at baptism and on Mount Tabor: Mark 9:7).

This guide *is to be found in faith*, as Peter found it, and when it is found Jesus rejoices: "Blessed are you, Simon . . . for flesh and blood has not revealed this to you" (Matthew 16:17). *And it is followed by love:* this is the first commandment.

Love *is will*, and by seeking out and accepting this will, the soul achieves identification with Christ. *Omnia mea tua sunt.* Identification leads to union, the final stage, the prelude to eternal union with God in Heaven. The bride brought into the garden in the Song of Songs, leaning on her bridegroom's arm, discovers and experiences the beginning of her spiritual life: *the Father*. In the bosom of the Father, where Jesus is a natural Son and the soul is one by adoption, the soul begins to experience its true childhood. *And this rebirth occurs in the Holy Spirit*. The Spirit came down into his Son on Mount Tabor, and he comes down into us so that we may discover Christ through faith. Diffused in our hearts, it leads us back, step by step, to a knowledge of God. *It guides us towards the truth in its entirety.* Indeed, it is the Trinity which is discovered deep in the centre of the soul.

Thus, not only does Jesus guide the soul to discover the mystery of God within it, but he wins it to eternal communion between the Divine Persons; (it becomes) a tiny drop of love drawn into an endless ocean. The Holy Spirit prepares the soul to emanate, in God, that same spirit of love – "an emanation of the Holy Spirit itself". "How may this be done?" "Father, I desire that those also, whom you have given me, may be with me where I am, to see my glory, which you have given me" (John 17:24) – which means, "That they may do in us – through sharing – the same thing that I do by my nature, which is to radiate the Holy Spirit."

Deeds

The climbing of Mount Carmel
The dark night
The spiritual canticle
The living flame
Spiritual maxims

Renunciation

Man's destiny is no longer to possess the earth but to possess Heaven. After his elevation to eternal life his vineyards, fields and houses should concern him less and less, as the vision of celestial wealth becomes increasingly vivid. In this continuous process of maturation which has renunciation as its reward, all that is human fades before the intensification of divine splendour. The Son of God trusts in the inheritance of the Father.

What interest can mortal benefits such as wealth and earthly glory have?

The sadness of a man condemned to die, and therefore to be forcibly separated from his treasures, is eclipsed by the new celestial reality. It is the answer to the final question in Ecclesiastes about the vanity of all things. The writer could not see the answer, for the time was not yet ripe, but he sensed that earthly goods cannot fully satisfy man. He was ruthless in his diagnosis, and he was right. His book is a refreshing transfusion of spirituality into the usual bourgeois Jewish idea of earthly enjoyment. St Paul completes the picture when he says what Solomon was not able to say.

Man's elevation to supernatural life, his official adoption into the family of God, completely changes the situation and consequently his dreams.

Therefore renunciation is simply an intelligent acceptance of death and its consequences, before it happens. Instead of relinquishing my houses, my possessions and my inheritance at the last moment, with no choice in the matter, I shall give them up now and consider myself, though still living on earth, to be a citizen of Heaven, a son of the Father, and I shall behave accordingly. I voluntarily renounce all my possessions, and by this act I declare my faith in the life to come and in those other blessings.

After renouncing material possessions comes the renunciation of intangible ones such as *"my point of view"*. At this point it is not difficult to understand how intelligent it is to accept another point of view – that of Christ. He who descended from Heaven is the only one who knows, and can recognize, the things of Heaven.

Above all (renunciation) is an act of humility and thus of truth.

Finally, a renunciation of the things of *the heart* is merely the acceptance of what will be after the resurrection of the flesh. All men will be God's angels.

St Vincent de Paul

This evening during vespers, after the umpteenth bad experience, my soul burst out in a heartfelt, ringing cry: "*Enough – I've understood! I don't want to have faith in myself any more!*"

How long and painful has been this path by which the Lord has led me to realize just how powerless I am! I must be exceptionally stubborn to have tried God's patience so sorely.

I don't want to make any more plans or promises which depend on this broken reed. My sole aspiration is expressed in this prayer: "*Lord, I place my trust in you, so that I may not be confounded.*" If I manage to keep to it, I'll be able to claim to have achieved something concrete. *God help me!*

21 July

> Providence of God the Father
> Providence of God the Son
> Providence of God the Holy Spirit
> Have mercy on me.

I believed in myself, I had hopes for myself and I achieved nothing. Now I only want to believe and put my hope in God. But how difficult it is to apply such a simple and thoroughly proven truth wholesale. Sin has truly overwhelmed us!

What we have to do to make progress is to be silent before God. The language which God understands best is silent *love*.

Look at God lovingly, without any desire to feel or understand anything definite coming from him. Keep spiritual calmness in your loving contemplation of God. Do you need to speak? Do it with that same calmness and peace (St John of the Cross).

Learn to keep looking at God with love, in tranquillity of spirit.

So, gradually and very soon, divine peace and repose will be infused into your soul, as well as an admirable and sublime knowledge of God, enfolded in divine love.

Having sought grace in your reading, you will find it in meditation; having been called to prayer, contemplation will be revealed to you.

In the end you will be examined on love; learn, then, to love God as he wishes to be loved and ignore the rest.

A task, however small, done in secret without wanting others to know about it, gives God more pleasure than a thousand things done to please other people.

The soul which walks in love neither feels nor causes weariness.

23 July

This evening, in the sweet glow of the liturgical celebration of St Mary Magdalene, the Child Jesus, back from Egypt, took me to a cave at the same altitude as Jerusalem but in the basin of the Dead Sea.

We prayed together and he celebrated Mass. He asked me to offer up the renunciation of every voluntary choice or deed of mine, down to the smallest thing, not dictated by the rule of the order. I accepted, sure of his help. I also agreed not to taste wine until the end of the novitiate, until I reach home. We will meet again. He made me realize how pleased he is with any task, even the smallest, done not to please other people, but for him alone. We must be satisfied with that.

24 July

"Any task, no matter how small, done only for him and not to be seen by other people . . ." (St John of the Cross).

"Whoever is dishonest in a very little is dishonest also in much" (Luke 16:10).

God is love.

My vocation is to love him. He is seeking me and I am seeking him. All creation is there before me, bearing his mark of love which speaks to me of him. The love-letter he has written me over the centuries is the Bible, and that too bears the mark of his love.

It is a jealous love.

To begin with, when I first met Jesus (love made flesh) we were friends. *I felt he was my friend.* Then, in the delirium of spiritual sickness, when he offered himself as medicine, I felt he was my brother. He gave his blood to heal me.

Later I knew him as a bridegroom. When love began to win me over, our free relationship of love intensified the human concept of marriage.

Now the relationship which I identify with most strongly, and which I care most about, is that of a son. After all, Jesus was a Son and so was the Word. By following Jesus, through the action of the Holy Spirit (which unites us to him in nuptual love), we reach the bosom of the Father: *"Where I am, there you may be also"* (John 14:3). *And in the bosom of the Father we begin our lives in the spirit of childhood – the spirit of a son. It is the ultimate relationship Jesus taught us: "Our Father".*

How will we react, then, when we realize, as St John of the Cross says, that in a sense we will emanate the Holy Spirit when in the bosom of the Father? *Our tiny drop of humanity immersed forever in the ocean of God!*

My God, I love you!

It is time to live as a son.

25 July

We have the spirit of adopted sons and not servants, in that the Spirit within us cries *"Abba, Pater."* *Matthew* (today), the eighth Sunday after Pentecost: "Is there anyone among you who, if your child asks for bread, will give a stone? . . . If you, therefore, being bad, are able to give good things to your children, how much more will your heavenly Father give good things to those who ask him!" (Matthew 7:9, 11). "I thank you, Father, Lord of heaven and earth, because you have hidden these things from the wise and the intelligent and have revealed them to infants" (Luke 10:21).

"And Jesus called a little child to him and put him in their midst and said: 'Truly I tell you, unless you change and become like children, you will never enter the kingdom of heaven. Whoever becomes humble like this child is the greatest in the kingdom of heaven' " (Matthew 18:2-4).

"Out of the mouths of babes and infants you have ensured perfect praise for yourself" (Psalm 8:2).

"Then he took a little child and put it among them; and taking it in his arms, he said to them. 'Whoever welcomes one such child in my name, welcomes me, and whoever welcomes me welcomes not me but the one who sent me' " (Mark 9:36-37).

"Is there anyone among you who, if your child asks for bread, will give a stone; or if your child asks for a fish, will give a snake instead of a fish? Or if the child asks for an egg, will give a scorpion? If you, then, who are evil, know how to give good gifts to your children, how much more will the heavenly Father give the Holy Spirit to those who ask him!" (Luke 11:11-13).

"Let the little children come to me, and do not stop them; for it is to such as these that the kingdom of God belongs. Truly I tell you, whoever does not receive the kingdom of God as a little child will never enter it" (Luke 18:16-17).

"But to all who received him, who believed in his name, he gave power to become children of God" (John 1:12).

26 July

St Anne. The furrow dug the day before yesterday by my divinely sent inspiration on life as a *son of God* becomes deeper all the time. *I have the feeling that this is a period of fundamental importance in my life.* Indeed, yesterday I experienced perhaps the most profound union with God of the whole novitiate. *I feel as if I were reborn,* and everything appears beautiful and joyful to me – even heavy labour on the building site. Five months like this, and my life will be transformed from top to bottom! God grant that it will be so!

31 July

Yet another month is over. Life in the novitiate passes swiftly and, for me, goes faster all the time. In five months' time I shall perhaps be travelling through the world with the great ideal of Nazareth in my heart, to be lived for the rest of my days.

All is going well, and even the heat is not as bad as I had feared.

I have switched from cobbling shoes to baking bread, with considerable advantages. That is another skill I can put under my belt.

My spiritual life is going well, especially after receiving the grace of understanding – or rather, experiencing – my status as a *son* of God. It feels permanent, not a temporary thing. God grant that it will be so.

Above all I feel more sure and in command of myself. In short, I can see better, and that was precisely the grace I had prayed so persistently for. It came as *an additional grace* on top of that greater and truly sublime one – that is, an awareness of God's paternity.

The hermitage at the Col is almost finished and we can already use the chapel. That will be a good thing, because at the moment – without the Eucharist – it is more difficult to concentrate. Now I realize what the presence of the Eucharist means, whereas once I would have fooled myself into thinking the opposite. Nature distracts me – given my well-known and deep love for it – and I am not yet capable of entering into intimacy with God with any ease. Today the Eucharist made it easier for me.

Let's go back to thoughts of the Father.

A father is his child's *origin, past, life, defence, strength, knowledge, intelligence, guide, light, safety, support, hope, possession and beginning. The child clings to him, places its hopes in him, expects everything from him, is safe with him and walks in his footsteps.*

If he is not there it trembles, without him it cries; if he returns it rejoices, and if it looks at him it is soothed. Life exists with him, and without him there is death. He is its father!

The child thinks of him even when not consciously doing so; it is with him even when alone, *it feels part of him always.*

Its father is admirable, strong, able to do anything. He knows everything and can do everything: he is its father.

The child glorifies, exalts and loves him: woe betide any who dare to criticize him: he is its father.

The baby clings tighter to its mother – the child to its father. The moment it reaches awareness, but is still little in every way, its father becomes the centre of its world.

That is why Jesus chose the child as an example: "Be like children."

He did not say: "Be like babies." A child has legs to walk with, but it can't manage it without its father. It is able to know and yet doesn't know; it is able to do and yet can't do.

The child is the true symbol of spiritual life and of our relationship with the Heavenly Father. Be like children. If you do not become as children . . .! Who will become like a child?

AUGUST 1955

3 August

I have made two commitments in this period of grace: (1) *a life of justice* in the everyday life of the novitiate; (2) *a life of faithfulness*, as described by St John of the Cross: "A task, however small, done in secret without wanting others to know about it, gives God more pleasure than a thousand things done to please other people." Yesterday a third commitment emerged: *compassion for my brothers*.

This is an up-to-date version of what Jesus said to the Pharisees: ". . . justice, mercy and faith. It is these you ought to have practised . . ." (Matthew 23:23).

Carlo the Pharisee should take careful note, and not forget so easily about:

> justice
> mercy
> faith

7 August

Today's reading from the Gospels (tenth Sunday after Pentecost) is Jesus' parable about the prayers of the Pharisee and the tax collector (Luke 18:9-14) – one of the most moving lessons in all the teaching of Jesus. By its light I must now analyze my prayers and see what needs to be corrected.

It is a fact that I feel, and tell God about, my unhappiness, my impotence and my faithlessness, but it is also a fact that deep inside I am proud of many – too many – things. I am proud, for example, of being a religious, of understanding God's affairs so well, of having a good line in piety. Also, I cannot deny my stubbornness as regards the apostolate and my presumptuousness over the problems of the Church and the future of the world.

I have something to say about both attitudes.

As regards the first, it only needs to be stressed. It is the truth and it doesn't take much to see the extent of my incapacity for good: I have so much experience at it that, I believe, there can be no doubt on the subject. However, this prayer, though true in itself, is sterile because it lacks faith in positive action on the part of God, the source of all good. The sight of the evil I am riddled with should immediately make me take refuge, not simply in an appeal to God, but in faith in his powerful and sure help.

Ample and incontrovertible proof of this can be found by reading all the prayers inspired by the Old and New Testaments. They have but one cry: "Lord, I trust in you."

I don't have this trusting faith. I shout: "Lord, I trust in you," but then I don't breathe life into it by trusting that God will answer me. Sometimes false humility leads me to doubt God's help. I really must mend my ways on this and doggedly nurture faith in his help. Moreover, I have had tangible proof of it recently. The Lord, I should add, does not respond straight away. He lets us insist for a while so that we can get our petition clear in our own minds, but then he comes, and his coming is truly life-giving.

As for my stubbornness and presumptuousness, I absolutely must stop being so pig-headed. I must give up my preconceived ideas, my pomposity about certain problems and the taint of pride in my ideas on the apostolate and on the apocalypse of the world. I need to be calmer, less cocksure, more silent.

In Jesus' parable the relationship between God and man, tainted by the Fall as he is now, is shown in terms of great simplicity.

The Lord is not surprised; indeed, he accepts as plain fact that man is sick and a sinner. The solution to that problem is to be found in prayer. "This man went down to his home justified . . ." (Luke 18:14). However, he specifies two basic conditions: a modest request and trusting prayer. Basically, it is man who has to become aware, and take stock of his situation and of God's function in this contingency. Man *who is not* appeals to *he who is*; man is sick, so he goes to a doctor; man cannot, so he asks someone *who can*.

God is truly the source: the source of life in creation, the source of salvation through redemption, the source of glorification in eternal life. It is up to man to understand whom he must rely on, whom he can expect something from, whom to turn to.

Each intention based on man's strength is doomed, but when it is founded on faith in God an intention is real and strong. Count on him, go to him, ask of him, hope in him, pray to him, beg him, believe in him.

This living faith is what brings God into contact with your weak and sick being. This is the strength to have absolute faith in: our strength, our "I can do anything if he upholds me".

Lord, I believe in you – you are my Creator, my redeemer, my everything. I want you, I love you. You are my life, my strength, my potential, my power, my hope and my faith. My everything. I love you, O Lord, and I ask you only to let me deeper into your thought, your plan and your will. Give me your command and then give me the strength to obey it. My nullity becomes strength in you; my incompetence, capability; and my very sin, a source of love.

You have solved everything for those who love you. Satan won't get the better of you, and nor will man. You'll win them over with your love, and even in your defeat there is far greater discomfiture for your enemy. You are truly God; you are the Son of God, Jesus; you are the life-giving Spirit, O Holy Spirit.

God, only God, all God, my light, my love, my everything. I am yours – make me more completely yours, for ever.

8 August

Yesterday, while thinking about Tomaselli,[1] ill and poor, and considering the answer to his problems from a spiritual point of view, I clearly saw the significance of total surrender to God. Impotent man, with no future, human hope or help – how can he save himself from despair? Learning not to make any more plans, not to defend oneself any more, not to search any longer, but to surrender oneself totally to God the Father's embrace by an act of absolute faith, means finding not only peace and serenity, but also the way to true sanctity.

Thinking about Domenico, at the end of the Salve Regina I suddenly thought: What about you? Why don't you follow this programme which you envisage so clearly for Domenico? With me it is not yet a case of illness or total helplessness, but it comes to the same thing – worse, in fact . . . And then the rest will follow. There are so few years left! Surrender your future, let your plans only be in him, don't be side-tracked, search for true peace, as in the lines you like so much: *"In your will lies our peace."* I must prepare myself for this act so that Charles' prayer will be a mystic reality, not a meaningless sound.

9 August
A worthy St Lawrence's Eve. My old pain is back, and in my suffering I feel once more all the instability and weakness of my devotion. How small I am! (Though not in the evangelical sense.) But how fiercely I have prayed, with faith this time, for the gift of knowing how to suffer!

This morning's prayer was unforgettable. I felt God like a mother with her nursing baby, like a father holding his child's hand; like riches, a bestower, a power-station, an Alpine lake, fruitfulness, food, breath, air and life.

My God, my Father, I love you.

12 August: St Clare
When you are within me, Lord, take the opportunity to change my heart. Replace my old, wooden, petty, selfish, poverty-stricken heart with your great, generous, sublime, beautiful, rich one. I am tired of the products of this poor, sick heart of mine and I would like to reawaken, feeling yours within me. Oh, how differently I would see the world! What sublime novelty there would be in everything! What zeal I would have before the Father! What compassion for my brothers!

Grant me this gift, O Jesus. When you come to me, draw very close and engulf and absorb me, as certain carnivorous plants do insects. Engulf this poor insect, convert me into your substance, your life.

I in you for ever.

"Go thou!"

A voice rings out in the world, which was created by the love of the Father and lost by the introduction of sin: "Go thou!"

And Jesus' mission began. Therefore the story begins with the Father; the earlier centuries were merely a preparation for this command and the later ones were a development of it. Jesus was sent: "Go thou!" Poor child – how this command echoed within him, in Egypt and when he came back. In Nazareth he heard the command: "Go thou!" That was the reason for the time when Jesus ran away, and for the harsh words he said to Mary and Joseph. "Go thou!"

His whole life was merely a contemplation of this sending – a preparation, a waiting, a time of thought, a quest for the Father's will in the depths of the abysses of truth. This is Jesus' essential attitude, his concern and his constant torment; *it is the proper attitude to every task*.

God grant me the gift of understanding, living and savouring this attitude, which was that of Jesus. "Go thou!" How everything would change. See how my past mistakes tremble in the light of this thought! Is that how I sought? Is that how I felt? That is why I was on the wrong track.

"Go thou!"

O Lord, by virtue of the obedience of Jesus, let me acquire this attitude, this humility, this obedience and this awareness. It seems that in every instant my first thought should be to seek out your will, which is the origin of every mandate, the truth in every action and the fruitfulness in each undertaking. "Go thou!"

The Eve of the Assumption

I am four months away from taking my vows, which means that all of eight months have gone by since I began my novitiate. It has been a period of fundamental importance in my life, a truly precious gift given me by Providence. My future and my vocation aside, finding myself here – cut cleanly off from my past and with the chance of making a complete revision – has powerfully contributed to the spiritual renewal of my soul. The most striking thing, I think, is that I have learnt to pray and have intensified my intimacy with God. My faith in Christ has grown and, above all, my love for the Father is greater. I must admit that here I have begun to feel myself to be a *son of God*, and to lay the foundations for a spirit of filiality. Another great advantage is that I have considerably changed the way in which I view the problems of the apostolate. Without a doubt *God is more present* to me and to the world.

From the ascetic point of view, I keep hearing in my head Jesus' reproof to the Pharisees: "You have neglected . . . justice and mercy and faith . . ." (Matthew 23:23). Just yesterday evening I shouted "Hypocrite!" at Carlo at the top of my voice, and my soul was filled with confusion.

Now my request to the Lord is very simple: "*Change my heart, replace mine with yours.*" It is the only way to get at the roots of my problems in order to solve them and, I believe, it is the only way to render the action of the Sacrament more efficacious.

Finally I have one thing to add. I discern love, with ever-increasing strength and abundance, at the hub of all human and divine affairs. It is truly the mover of all things, the key to all mysteries, the inspiration towards all that is good. God is a God of love; Paradise is the enjoyment of love; love is the goal as well as the source. In this light behold creation, the Incarnation, the death of Jesus, the Eucharist, the forgiving of souls and their glorification.

Deus charitas est (1 John 4:8).

18–19 August
Retreat at the Col: unforgettable days. Theme: continuous prayer. I asked for the grace to be able to *pray twenty-four hours a day* and to manage never to lose touch with God; to explore the concept of *"live with Jesus in the bosom of the Father"*; to combine the two in one, and create a way of life from it. At this point the meaning of *true confidence in God, as the sum of faith, hope and love*, springs spontaneously to life. In any case, how can one possibly guide oneself in such unfathomable matters? That is why one must uproot the weed of self-conceit, of the ego which wants to see where it is going, and all such things – things poisoned by pride. Total self-surrender is, once again,

the most rational attitude to take, and the most suitable one for a child in its father's arms.

Eleventh Sunday after Pentecost

What is written in the Law? "You shall love the Lord your God with all your heart, and with all your soul, and with all your might" (Deuteronomy 6:4-5), and love your neighbour as yourself. Do this and you shall live.

In order to have life, which is God himself, one must love. It is the vocation of all, and my vocation too. I have asked it of the Lord, I ask it now, I shall ask it in the future: I want it to become real in me. I want to suffer every time I stray from prayer and from him. That is the gift I have asked for, and he must give it me out of his love. After all, it is he who wants it, and I am only asking him for what he already wants. O Lord, I want your will so that you may do mine. These are the rules of love. God encourages tastes in us that are his tastes, and then he makes us ask for them, and in granting them to us he satisfies us and does what he cannot help doing: his divine will. That is what happens with love!

God, my God, let me always know your will; let me ardently desire it, and then grant it to me so that you may be glorified in it.

Then I shall be blessed, as you truly say in your crowning sermon (Matthew 5:1-12):

Blessed are the poor in spirit,
for theirs is the kingdom of heaven.
Blessed are those who mourn,
for they will be comforted.
Blessed are the meek,
for they will inherit the earth.
Blessed are those who hunger and thirst for righteousness,
for they will be filled.
Blessed are the merciful,
for they will receive mercy.
Blessed are the pure in heart,

for they will see God.
Blessed are the peacemakers,
for they will be called children of God.
Blessed are those who are persecuted for righteousness' sake,
for theirs is the kingdom of heaven.
Blessed are you when people revile you and persecute you . . .
    on my account . . .
for your reward is great in heaven.

Blessed are 1. the poor
            2. those who mourn
            3. the meek
            4. those who hunger and thirst for righteousness
            5. the merciful
            6. the pure in heart
            7. the peacemakers
            8. the persecuted

This is a profile of the son, the child who was so pleasing to Jesus that he encouraged us to emulate it if we want to enter the Kingdom.

Distance the heart from earthly possessions, imitate the poverty of Jesus, become poor for love of the poor, do not respond to violence and accept the consequent suffering, be just and love justice, accept persecution for love of Jesus. My God, grant that I may succeed in emulating this portrait of your son. I am so far from it! You can do anything – trace in me those features you love so much! *Is this your will? Your will be done.*

28 August

The whole universe spins around an axis which is not the physical one, or one represented by the history of mankind: the true axis of the spiritual universe is the Father and his Son.

Therefore do away with all illusion and false perspectives. The quest for God, for his love and his adoration, is man's essential duty on earth. All the rest truly counts for very little!

I have asked the Lord for these things: *a change of heart, the spirit of perpetual prayer, his ever more intimate revelation, and the life of the beatitudes.*

The Beheading of St John the Baptist

My greatest friend in Heaven has not forgotten that I have become a novice in a new life, very close to his way of thinking and to his erstwhile earthly attachments. Today, unexpectedly, he brought me a present, a big present worthy of him.

During adoration he entrusted me with that beautiful little boy from Nazareth called Jesus. "Take care of him," he told me. "Hold him close. Feed him, watch over him at night, cover him up, but above all love him." I hugged him in my arms, weeping with love. I shall never let him go without, and I will always give him a share of my food so that my little penitence may have a name and a love.

I shall always take him with me, and my life will be a copy of his in Nazareth. It will be easy for me to know what it was like, because he will show me. We shall always pray to the Father and the Holy Spirit, the Madonna and St Joseph together. I think of myself as an errand boy in St Joseph's workshop.

My life with Jesus will always be sweet. Thank you, Father! Thank you, John the Baptist! Thank you, Mary!

"Our Father": When teaching us to pray, Jesus began by giving us a relationship with God, calling him by the name of Father. This is the most exalted relationship which exists in love, and it is also the call of the family to the spirit of filiation which was so dear to him: "unless you . . . become like children" (Matthew 18:3).

"Hallowed be your name": May you be known, O Father. That will suffice. Make yourself known, and everyone will follow you, do your will and enter into your Kingdom. *Indeed, Jesus himself will tell you: "This is eternal life – that they know you, Father."*

"Give us this day our daily bread": A simple, human prayer, far from the needless complications of pseudo-mystics. "I am hungry, Father: give me what I need."

Then, as it grows, the child becomes aware that what it does is not always good. Evil is a sad reality, and so, *"forgive us our debts as we also have forgiven our debtors"*. It is already done. Along the same lines, Jesus says: "If you do not forgive . . ." (cf. Matthew 7:2).

"Do not bring us to the time of trial": Jesus does not teach us a lofty, self-assured prayer – quite the opposite, in fact.

And this is the point at which the childlike soul is invited to say: "I know that in order to grow I need conflict and trials but . . . go gently Father – I am small."

The marriage at Cana (John 2:1-11). This event occupies a middle position between private life with the family of Nazareth, and public life. This is the first act of faith made to Jesus by his disciples. The Madonna, who still feels very close to her son, is there with her faith in the power and even more in the thought of God. Her instruction is awe-inspiring, all-encompassing and programmatic: *"Do whatever he tells you."*

Our Father *in Heaven*. Where is God if not in every place? Is not *Heaven* in every place, then? Is every place not a *hidden* place, where he hides himself and where we seek him out?

Is Heaven not the vast world of the stars where he hides himself with his power and his beauty? Is Heaven not the mystery of the infinitely small: the atom?

Is Heaven not a flower? Is Heaven not the earth with its maternal fruitfulness? And the sea, and the plants? And the instinct of the bird, which travels thousands of kilometres without knowing the way? Every created thing is an immense, incredibly beautiful, peaceful and harmonious Heaven, where God hides himself with his power, his love and his beauty. His love above all.

And the heart of man? What a wondrous and sublime Heaven – doubly Heaven, mysterious Heaven. That is why the Father mentions "Heavens" and not "Heaven".[2] There are many, an infinite number, of Heavens, and it has been given to me, man, to seek them out and to reveal, worship, talk with and "sanctify" my Creator in them; to discover his holiness, in other words. *Our Father in Heaven.*

SEPTEMBER 1955

3 September

Lord, give me a new heart, give me your heart. Can't you see how sick mine is? Selfishness, pettiness, impurity, injustice, pride and superficiality are all products of this old root, sprung from the far older stock of my ancestors. How is it possible to love with a new heart? You said to Nicodemus: "You must be born from above" (John 3:7), but what is your plan, your design? What must I do to get my old self to go into a decline and die? How should I view this new reality which you have instilled in me by your grace? Help me to understand and, even more, to live your sweet will for us – we who are redeemed by your precious blood.

God's plan

"Blessed be the God and Father of our Lord Jesus Christ, who has blessed us in Christ with every spiritual blessing in the heavenly places, just as he chose us in Christ before the foundation of the world to be holy and blameless before him in love. *He destined us for adoption as his children* through Jesus Christ, according to the good pleasure of his will, to the praise of *his glorious grace that he freely bestowed on us in the Beloved*. In him we have redemption through his blood, the forgiveness of our trespasses, according to the riches of his grace that he lavished on us. With all wisdom and insight he has made known to us the mystery of his will, according to his good pleasure that he set forth in Christ, as a plan for the fullness of time, *to gather up all things in him, things in heaven and things on earth*" (Ephesians 1:3-10).

How will this plan be carried out after man's betrayal? How can this new reality be made to spring from, and grow on, the old stock of humanity, which has reverted to the wild state? He said to

Nicodemus: *"No one can enter the kingdom of God without being born of water and Spirit"* (John 3:5). So we have to be born again, and in very particular conditions: "To all . . . who believed in his name, *he gave power to become children of God, who were born, not of blood or of the will of the flesh or of the will of man, but of God"* (1:12–13).

It is a genuine rebirth, but one that neither man nor woman has anything to do with. *The new begetting comes from God himself,* and the new-born spiritual being *is a child of God.*

Thus a new life begins; a child which is born to God, an adopted child of the Most High, destined as it grows *"to be conformed to the image of his Son, in order that he might be the firstborn within a large family"* (Romans 8:29).

How this happens is part of the mystery of the grace diffused within us by the Holy Spirit.

How can we imagine it? Jesus compares it to the life of a vine, Paul to the lymph in a body. It remains a mystery, and even though the idea of a graft onto an old olive tree, and the concept of fire transforming iron, may help us to form a picture, it eludes us. Everything which this adoption by God entails within us, is infinitely beyond our comprehension.

St John, who, together with St Paul, was perhaps the one who came closest to understanding this mystery, defines the new life as *"eternal life"*.

"Whoever believes in the Son has eternal life" (John 3:36), and he uses the same words as those which Jesus said to the Father in order to explain the meaning of eternal life: "This is eternal life, that they may know you, the only true God, and Jesus Christ, whom you have sent" (17:3).

Therefore it is a life which develops with an ever-deeper awareness of God.

Again, it is John who discusses this development, on that momentous night of love and betrayal.

"They who have my commandments and keep them are those who love me; and those who love me will be loved by my Father, and I will love them and reveal myself to them" (John 14:21).

Jesus will reveal himself to God's adopted child, and in revealing himself he will reveal the Father, because "whoever has seen me has seen the Father" (John 14:9).

The increasing number of such revelations has the effect of making the adopted child conform ever more closely to the image of God's natural Son: Jesus.

This is the way.

The soul is impatient: "A thorn was given me in the flesh, a messenger of Satan to torment me, to keep me from being too elated . . . Three times I appealed to the Lord about this, that it would leave me, but he said to me, 'My grace is sufficient for you, for power is made perfect in weakness.' So, I will boast all the more gladly of my weaknesses, so that the power of Christ may dwell in me. Therefore I am content with weaknesses, insults, hardships, persecutions, and calamities for the sake of Christ; for whenever I am weak, then I am strong" (2 Corinthians 12:7-10).

That is exactly what I need – I who am so swift to ask God to take away my troubles, my weaknesses and my infirmities.

When will I begin to understand that being in trouble is man's true condition, and that he must accept it, love it and offer it up? When will I learn to boast about my weaknesses? When, having recognized them, I learn to accept them and offer them up as the raw material for Christ to act upon.

This is what he wants from man. He is the Creator, the Recreator, the Omnipotent. His is the strength, the greatness, the perfection. God "is here for this", he is the *"restorer"*, the doctor. What would a doctor do if the hospitals were empty? He needs full hospitals. The more serious the case, the more it is *his*; the more complicated it is, the more his power blazes forth.

God, give me the grace to *understand* this, and to love and accept it.

4 September

What counts most – to praise God or to love him? First of all *love* – that's certain. Then praise emerges as a response to love.

And why, I asked myself today, does God want us to love him?

Why does he make a commandment of it, and the first one too? Today the answer came to me clearly. Because he wants us in his family, and how is family life possible without love? It is love which binds, shelters, explains and understands. It is love which brings peace, joy, rejoicing and a sense of eternity. It is love which builds, makes fruitful and bestows life. It is everything: it is God himself. It is his innermost secret. It is his life.

All the rest stems from this. What good is there in gaining the whole world if it is not pleasing to this love? In working or even dying for the sake of good if it is not for this love? This love is his will. To do his will means satisfying this love.

That is the unifying core of your life! That is what you absolutely have to achieve, and once you have achieved it, you must never lose it again. God's will, which means God's love.

O Lord, give me your love. I ask it in the name of your Son, Jesus. Give me a mountain of it. Nothing else matters any more. Let me live for love and, even more, die for love. Let me burn with love like a sacrificial goat engulfed in flame on the altars of long ago; let me be permeated with love, like Jesus on the cross. Is that too much to ask? I know I am only asking what you want, your holy will, expressed in your own commandment: "You shall love the Lord your God with all your heart, and with all your soul, and with all your mind" (Matthew 22:37). Lord, do your will in me: give me your love, lots and lots and lots and lots and lots and lots of it.

8 September
One must present oneself at the feast of the Holy Name of Mary with a soul prepared to surrender totally to the will of God. This is the thought which came to me today as I prayed.

The Eve of the Holy Name of Mary
The inspiration to get ready to offer up my will on the feast-day of the Madonna appears to me to be genuine. Over these past few days this thought has been at the heart of my adoration. Today is the eve,

and I am now ready to make my gift. This is how I would describe it in the form of a prayer:

My God, here I am in your presence. I am a small and wretched thing but I am your creature. That which is good in me you placed there with your love; that which is bad is the fruit of my sins and the sins of my fathers.

You created me for love, as you created the universe. You are love. Your plan was dictated by your fatherhood, and it was already clear before you at the Creation. You envisaged us all in Christ and, as if inspired by the joyous beauty of this Father-Son relationship of yours, you wanted us to share in it too as your adopted children in him. You were setting up a family – and hence the first commandment: "You shall love the Lord your God with all your heart, and with all your soul, and with all your mind" (Matthew 22:37).

It is obvious: family life is based on love and would be impossible without it. That, then, is the reason for your loving command, "You shall love." Yes, O Father, we must love you because it is good, it is beautiful, it is joyful to do so. Loving you is eternal life; it is the relationship within the family which you created and which you want to be yours for all time.

That being so, it follows that the first law derived from love is "Do the will of the beloved." We must do your will because it is the only way to show our love, and because it is the source of yet more love.

In this belief, Father, I stand before you and declare: I want to obey your will forever. I want it to be the rule guiding my life, my compass along the way, the inspiration behind my deeds.

But since it would have neither meaning nor, what is more important, force without your love, I have to have that too. I ask you this, safe in the knowledge that it is your will: Father, give me your love and I will give you my will. I already love you a little; multiply this little to infinity and I shall be satisfied.

I know I am asking something good, I know I am asking the right thing, but you are the one who has made me realize it. Love is everything. Love is the key to all mysteries, the solution to all divine enigmas, the motive behind your every action. You are love; love is life eternal.

You created for love and, divine artist that you are, you gazed upon your creature with joy. You love this creature. It is a moral law, not a physical one, and you predisposed your creation to good, because you are holy. Your creation, the universe, is truly a holy thing. You are the Holy One because you want good, and your holiness impels you towards it because goodness is the fruit of love. We spoiled your masterpiece through disobedience and you sent Jesus to mend your shattered work. The act of restoration was in itself a new creation, and it surpassed the first one in beauty. You are truly love.

Now everything is headed towards the final act: glorification, the establishing of everything in Christ, the supreme family life you wanted.

I ask you, then, for the gift of this new life – your love – and I'll give you my will in exchange. You know me and you know my worthlessness. Therefore it would be pointless for you to take my will first. Too often I have shown that I don't want to exercise my will; so give me your love, and I am certain that for love I shall do what you want. It is my vocation – you know that. Like Peter, I am ready to throw myself in the water if I see you. But I am also ready to say, "I don't know him" when the cold night air has cooled my ardour.

God, you know me – don't let me fall again. Always win me over with love. I shall be yours. Besides, it is truth and self-knowledge which has made me sure that I am a poor thing, a piece of rusty iron.

However, your love, which I now know, has made me understand that even rusty iron turns to flame in the fire. That is the answer to everything – *fire*. It will seal the stinking mouth of my grave and the foul vapours will no longer offend. It will transform iron, and give new meaning to the wretched state of my being. Do you agree, Lord? Shall we sign a pact? Give me your love and I shall give you my will – all of it.

Your own Carlo

The Stigmata of St Francis

Gifts arrive on given dates . . . and even more arrive unexpectedly. After a few days of aridity, during adoration today the Lord, in all his power and gentleness, made himself heard: "It is time to begin the final assault on your ego," he told me, and he showed me the wretched state of my soul, which always concentrates on itself.

How shining truth is when it is *his*! How easily errors are brought to light when he uncovers them! My God, do not let me down – remember our pact. You know I put myself in your hands. How strongly I now feel that without you I am nothing, and totally incapable of the slightest good deed!

25 September

These days are rather empty, except for an increasing awareness of my wretchedness.

I answered the clear summons to the fight against myself with days of evasion and distraction. My devotion is too tied up with my feelings, and what is more serious, it is always on the look-out for pleasure.

I must brace myself, go back to the points I have mulled over lately and put them into effect:

1. Surrender of self to God.
2. The struggle against my ego.
3. A conscious acceptance of the cross.

If I can manage to shift my devotion onto the fulcrum of will and to measure it by the yardstick of the cross, it will without doubt be the biggest step forward I shall ever have taken in my life.

God assist me with his grace!

Texts on sacrifice and the struggle against self

"Blessed are the poor . . . Blessed are those who mourn . . . Blessed are those who hunger and thirst for righteousness" (Matthew 5:3-4, 6);

"If any want to become my followers, let them deny themselves" (Matthew 16:24).

"Whoever wishes to be first among you must be your slave" (Matthew 20:26).

"Whoever wishes to be first among you must be slave of all" (Mark 10:44).

"If your right hand causes you to sin, cut it off" (Matthew 5:30).

"Unless a grain of wheat falls into the earth and dies . . ." (John 12:24).

"Those who love their life lose it, and those who hate their life in this world will keep it for eternal life" (John 12:25).

"But we have this treasure in clay jars, so that it may be made clear that this extraordinary power belongs to God and does not come from us. We are afflicted in every way, but not crushed; perplexed, but not driven to despair; persecuted, but not forsaken; struck down, but not destroyed; always carrying in the body the death of Jesus, so that the life of Jesus may also be made visible in our bodies" (2 Corinthians 4:7-11).

". . . in honour and dishonour, in ill repute and good repute. We are treated as imposters, and yet are true; as unknown, and yet are well known; as dying, and yet are alive; as punished, and yet are not killed; as sorrowful, yet always rejoicing; as poor, yet making many rich; as having nothing, and yet possessing everything" (2 Corinthians 6:8-10).

"I will not boast, except of my weaknesses" (2 Corinthians 12:5).

"For he was crucified in weakness, but lives by the power of God. For we are weak in him, but . . . we will live with him by the power of God" (2 Corinthians 13:4).

"I have been crucified with Christ" (Galatians 2:19).

"May I never boast of anything except the cross of our Lord Jesus Christ, by which the world has been crucified to me, and I to the world" (Galatians 6:14).

"I want to know Christ and the power of his resurrection and the sharing of his sufferings by becoming like him in his death" (Philippians 3:10).

"I am completing what is lacking in Christ's afflictions" (Colossians 1:24).

26 September

This morning I kissed the heart of the Father and I heard the voice

of the Son. The Father has the same heart as the Son. The same love.
I thought about my vocation to live as Jesus did as a child, searching
for his feelings and prayers. How wonderful! All the beatitudes beat
in that small boy's heart. Poverty, gentleness, purity, tears, a thirst
for justice, peace and suffering.

I saw the boy Jesus climb the mountain on which Abraham was
invited to make his sacrifice. Jesus took the place of Isaac. When he
reached the top the Father struck him with all the anger roused by
sin. The poor boy was wearing the mask of all the sins of humanity.

Poor Jesus! Poor Father! You didn't want Abraham to kill Isaac,
but you struck your own Son.

What a superabundance of love for us! What a price for the Father
and Son to have to pay! How immense divine love is! But I felt Jesus'
pain. It wasn't so much the physical pain of the blows as the sight
of the Father's angry face, and the horrible price of the sin that he
was carrying. Seen in that light, Psalm 21 comes to life. It was Jesus'
prayer.

O God, give me your love, give me full awareness of the weight
of your cross! Let me die for love!

> Live the life of Jesus as a boy.
> Pray as if I were him.
> Act in his name.
> Love the Father as he does.

Today, before the Holy Sacrament, I felt a desire to invoke God
as the strength to draw on in my weakness. Then I called him the
Sun, and I basked in his rays. Then came the litany, and I called him
Heaven – Air – Star – Wind – Firmament – Sea – Land – Flower
– Field – Bread – Wine – Oil – Wheat – Tree . . . I could not stop
because everything he had created had something of him – his beauty,
his goodness and his love – in it.

Make me your son, O Father. Make me your son, O Son. Make
me your son, O Holy Spirit.

I want to live in your house as a son, O Father; I want to eat your bread, drink your wine, enjoy your peace. When a son is true, all the beatitudes become a reality in him: poverty, meekness, peace, tears, justice and a thirst to suffer for the Father.

Father, make me your son; Son, make me your son; Holy Spirit, make me your son.

OCTOBER 1955

7 October

If I were to sum up all God's works in one simple but appropriate image, I would compare them to the building of a house in the country and to the way of life there.

A hill, a vineyard, an olive grove, some fields, a meadow or two and a hedge. Up on the hill is an old country house, simple and spacious, airy and full of the scent of baking bread. The house of the Father, the house of bread.

And this is the house where I have been invited to come and live as a son.

What law regulates the entire household? Love, simplicity, faith in the Father, work, love for one's brothers, peace – above all peace, infinite peace.

I have all I need to sustain life: bread, wine and oil. But more than all else, I have the love of my Father. How complete this love is; it is the most all-encompassing, most human, most free, most welcome love of all.

God chose the image of love between Father and Son as an image of his love and ours.

God made it his: Our Father.

He made it into a prayer: Our Father.

Degree of relationship: Our.

Eternal echo of love: Our Father.

23 October

This is the time of the wrong injection[1] – a time of trial, a time of faith, a time of suffering, a time of prayer.

This is what I have thought during this period:

Jesus is *God's humility*.

The God of love comes down to me in a way which is dictated by his infinite humility: "Learn from me; for I am gentle and humble in heart" (Matthew 11:29).

Humility is truly one of the most mysterious and profound attributes of infinite holy perfection. Only love can understand it, and without love it is impossible to accept. A Muslim could never understand such a thing. To us who believe in love, humility means total, trusting surrender.

To empty oneself of self, to lose all self-esteem, to obliterate oneself, to become very small: that is the way to get God to fill us and act powerfully in us.

Moreover, Jesus says we need the life of *a son*, the life of a child, in order to enter the Kingdom.

Only by being small can one live the beatitudes to their full extent, because only when one is small is one poor, meek, thirsty, hungry, merciful and able to give everything for justice and the Father.

During these days of trial all the instability and fragility of my spiritual make-up has surfaced. How far I am from that true faith which never loses its calmness or its peace at any time!

What an effort it took me to accept, to say "Yes"!

But the moment I said "Yes", what blinding light! Faith really is the greatest act of homage one can render to the Creator! To feel oneself immersed in God's loving presence, and to lose all notion of visible things in the light shed by invisible ones. Believe, believe, believe, believe – always. Believe despite everything, and love, despite the frost which afflicts you when you are alone and you feel abandoned by God and by other people. To see God and his action in everything and never doubt his omnipotence and his love, to surrender oneself trustingly to his work as redeemer, brother and Father.

A scene: my dying aunt's[2] concern about problems at the stable. How would I measure up in the same circumstances?

I imagine my ill aunt climbing towards home from Viola. How would you hope to live the same experience? Her thoughts? The earth and the sky – blindness?

It is strange how easily we spy opportunities for faith in others. But when it is our turn we become blind and tremble more than anyone else. It is then that the whole of the mechanism intended to cope with trials ought to take over. My God, what a wretch I am!

Christ spent the night praying to God. What mystery there is in his prayer! The prayer of the great and only worshipper.

"He called to him those whom he wanted" (Mark 3:13): the freedom of God. We don't give enough thought to the fact that we depend on this freedom of the Lord and on his approval.

"All in the crowd were trying to touch him" (Luke 6:19), because a power came out of him. One day, faced with the problem of faith, that same crowd was to abandon him. And he commanded them not to reveal that they had been healed.

Jesus does not look for popularity – he knows it's worth nothing and he does not want to sway crowds. He is aware of the age-old temptation of miracle-making. He seeks the truth – he knows it will spread.

Matthew comments on Jesus' method in the words of Isaiah: "Here is my servant, whom I uphold, my chosen, in whom my soul delights" (Isaiah 42:1). *"He will not cry"* (42:2). Jesus proclaims the truth with discretion, peacefully. He doesn't set himself up as a popular leader; he is not after personal success.

"A bruised reed he will not break" (42:3): the divine patience of the Master as he waits: a lesson for our prideful and uncaring haste.

The Feast of Christ the King
Milad spoke about Jesus' royalty:

Jesus is the perfect man. Total divinity resides in him. Sent by the Father, he was given all power in Heaven and on Earth.

He is the leader and the Father sees all mankind embodied in him. He is an authentic King but, as it says in the collect, his Kingdom is "one of truth and life, of holiness and grace, of justice, love and peace". All the peoples of the earth are summoned to this Kingdom and Christ was sent for all.

Where there is truth and life, holiness and grace, justice, love and peace, there is his Kingdom.

We must completely change our mentality, bogged down as it is in the concept of "sectarian Christianity", "us and them"; this attitude might have had its uses in other times, but it is not applicable to today's world.

The visible Church is the repository of the whole message of treasure, grace and the sacraments, but Christ's action does not end there. Each person who comes into this world is illuminated by Christ, prepared by him to receive a revelation which becomes steadily brighter. For this reason Christ is the King of all peoples and the Sovereign of all humanity.

Therefore let us rid our thoughts of the concept of separateness, which arises from hatred or from misconceptions, pride, incomprehension and, at times, injustice and a lack of love.

Everything must be viewed in the light of the great Kingdom which is continually expanding, in depth and in breadth. Good will towards all peoples, open-mindedness towards all men and a quest for the truth in every part of the earth.

NOVEMBER 1955

All Saints' Day

Arturo took his vows. Milad gave a talk on the beatitudes. My leg is paralyzed[1] – a lesson in humility. The beatitudes illustrate God's taste in humanity, which he created and redeemed. Even without sin the Lord would have told us: "Be poor, be meek and be peacemakers."

There is one of God's mysteries to be discovered in each beatitude, a mystery completely hidden from our eyes by sin.

Blessed are they who have *the heart of a poor man*, was Milad's interpretation; like Jesus, who is the eternal master of all perfection. A poor person is one who does not prize possessions, doesn't feel superior to others and who knows he depends on God for everything.

Poverty brings meekness with it, an expression of true humility, and this humility rouses hunger and thirst for justice.

In this attitude the soul thirsts for forgiveness, and the sight of its own faults, and its compassion, do away with all desire to judge others: "Blessed are the merciful".

In this light the spiritual life prepares the soul to achieve "purity of heart". No more shadows, no more pockets of selfishness: everything is pure in the light of God.

And God's Son, the supreme gift, is bestowed: the bringer of peace. The bringer of peace is he who combines the man of peace and the Prince of Peace, and spreads God's supreme gift, "peace to all men", around him.

The beatitudes would have ended here if it had not been for sin. But this terrible reality not only brought Jesus, the perfect man, to earth, but also Jesus crucified.

And this is the most exalted beatitude of all: emulation of the suffering Christ: "Blessed are you when people revile you and persecute

you and utter all kinds of evil against you falsely on my account . . ."
(Matthew 5:11).

Jesus, grant me the spirit of the beatitudes.

Milad on prayer

It is a search for God.

Only the beatific vision of God will remove this fundamental characteristic from prayer.

Prayer begins when the soul makes contact with God by a profound act, an act of concentration which is like a match lighting a fire. The more deeply such an act "offers up self", the truer and more valid it is.

It is not a question, then, of a wealth of ideas or feelings, but the wealth of one's gifts. Indeed, in this sense, true prayer becomes progressively simpler. A perfect example of this is the tax collector's prayer as compared to the long-windedness of the Pharisee's prayer.

Therefore it is *truth* which counts, and it is the most genuine, most effective and most real prayer of all.

After this initial act, and having established contact with God through its willingness to give, the soul embarks on its prayer.

There is no given method for it, because the freedom of the spirit holds sway. Some people expand on the act by praying out loud, and some prefer silent prayer. The value of vocal prayer certainly should not be underestimated, because it too is capable of expressing the soul's donation and of developing it along the same lines.

The Feast of St Charles

Decidedly, my patron saint has begun to take an interest in me. St Charles' Day 1954[2] brought me the gift of my vocation as a Little Brother. St Charles' Day 1955 has brought me the gift of a deeper understanding of prayer. Milad's words have lit a great light inside me. Thoughts have been brought to life and are no longer just abstract theory as they were before.

The divine life within us

The great, boundless gift of the Father, the mystery of love hidden over the centuries, revealed to us in the fullness of time and won for us by Jesus, is that we too will share in divine life. "To all . . . who believed in his name, he gave power to become children of God" (John 1:12).

Becoming God's children means starting to live a new life, which is the life of God within us: a life as God's children. This life is created in "Christ Jesus". That is how the Father saw and sees us – in his beloved Son. Jesus is the life in the Mystic Body of which he is also the head. "I am the vine, you are the branches" (John 15:5): that is the way to live this life. "Abide in me as I abide in you. Just as the branch cannot bear fruit by itself unless it abides in the vine, neither can you unless you abide in me" (15:4). We can claim, then, that the divine life within us is the lymph which flows from our head, Jesus, and circulates through our being. In the final analysis it is *the life of Jesus in us*, the life of the Son, the true Son who has his prayer, his action and his sacrifice.

This is where *true prayer*, the true apostolate and our true identification with the Passion of Christ spring from. Let Jesus pray – that is supernatural prayer, the sort that counts. Let Jesus act – that is the true, effective, overwhelming apostolate.

From now on I must model my life on these truths. They must be the real inspiration for *"becoming small"*, for not valuing *human resources, wealth, one's own action* or one's own *being*. Given the vast disproportion between the *divine life within me and my own life*, which must take precedence?

Everything has to be done again, thought through again. What errors of judgement have been committed in the so-called apostolate! *The more man predominates* in the apostolate, the less truth is in it; and the more Jesus is in evidence, the more truth is in it. The episode in which Jesus sends Peter to Cornelius is *the way* of true divine action (Acts 10).

Jesus, give me the grace to live your prayer, your action and your sacrifice.

Milad on prayer

Being a supernatural organism, a soul imbued with sanctifying grace becomes capable of supernatural acts. Divine life in us is the lymph which flows from the divine life of Jesus.

However, since we are both body and soul, we need supernatural forces to invest all our natural faculties. These are the virtues – the theological virtues above all: faith, hope and charity. Then come the others: prudence, justice, strength and temperance complete the range of supernatural forces which invest natural ones. *These forces are controlled by our initiative*, and if we don't let them act they stay inert, like shipped oars in a boat. However, that boat has sails, which are the gifts of the Spirit. But their action depends on the divine wind and on the divine wind alone. Where is prayer to be found in such an organism? *In the theological virtues of faith, hope and charity*. If it is not there, then it is not true prayer.

Fr Charles de Foucauld defined prayer as "thinking of God with love", and it is a good definition. Also, his method of taking the *person* of Jesus, and not stray thoughts, as his starting-point, is an extremely reliable one. True prayer requires *two* participants: the one praying and the one who is being prayed to – God. Then there is freedom to choose one's way of praying: feelings speak – anything can serve to strike the spark. But . . . when possible, it is better to strip oneself of everything human in favour of the spiritual, in faith, hope and love.

14 November

The last month of the novitiate is beginning. Pietro[3] will come and so, perhaps, will a few friends. My leg still won't support me, it is cold at the Col, and there are lots of other things of the same ilk. I ought to make a real effort to conclude this period with flying colours. There is no doubt that it has been a positive one, but if I had been more generous it could have been far more efficacious.

More clarity, more truth, more humility, more love. And that's not all.

As usual, I am counting on some divine gift to make up for my shortcomings.

The day after tomorrow I am due to begin the novena for Antonio's recovery.[4]

The return from Béni Abbès (Précis of Milad)

The core of Charles de Jésus' spirituality is his personal friendship with Jesus and his all-absorbing imitation of Jesus' life.

Charles had no established plan; his only beacon was "to do his will, seek out his will, worship his will" (Milad).

"Do not judge, so that you may not be judged . . . Why do you see the speck . . .?" (Matthew 7:1, 3). How can we eradicate this terrible evil of judgement we have in us? Jesus himself commands us, in the strongest possible terms, not to judge our brothers. It is humanly impossible, and only the intervention of the Holy Spirit can perform the miracle. Only when the beatitude of mercy has filled us will this masterpiece of love – not judging others – be possible.

For our part, it is an insoluble problem, and the world is proof of this – the religious world included. *Judging* is the sower of the seed of discord which devastates the field of God.

Actually, the Lord doesn't mean this command to make us blind. We must judge actions and we can judge opinions: but not people.

We don't know. We are faced with a mystery when confronted with man and, what is more, we are also dealing with another exalted mystery: that of God's freedom.

None of us can know the future, the virtues, the holiness of one of our brothers. Lukewarm men have changed and overtaken those more virtuous than they. And then, who can know what anyone else is responsible for or what they are guilty of? So the Lord's command is quite clear.

But, as we were saying, the Holy Spirit provides the true solution by implanting the wealth of the beatitude of mercy in us.

The light which shines from this sublime beatitude sheds great clarity on the soul's own wretchedness, and thus it loses all desire to judge others and asks only for mercy, mercy, mercy.

22 November (Milad)
"Do not throw your pearls before swine" (Matthew 7:6). First of all, we must bear the coarseness of the Semitic language in mind. Secondly, we must apply a comparison invented to fit a different situation.

Here Jesus is telling those who have a message to deliver to be discreet, to use a little strategy and to adapt the fare to suit the stomachs of their audience.

"You will know them by their fruits" (Matthew 7:16). That is how man should be judged: afterwards. His deeds are what count, not his words. This method is truly infallible.

"The good person out of the good treasure of the heart produces good" (Luke 6:45). Until he speaks he may well fool others, but it is hard for him not to give himself away if there are bad things in his treasure. They will emerge, and in the end he will be judged on what is revealed.

How pointless it is to try, especially where charity is concerned, to smother only the visible shoot of the plant with smiles, soothing words and attempts at patience (a true Phariseeism extremely common among Christians). It is far better to pull it up by the roots and deal with it in depth, down where man keeps his treasure. Then charity truly becomes possible: when *an effort to love* has been made, without deceit and snide allusions.

Just think of the weeds shooting up in Rome!

23 November

Jesus brings a spirit of freedom to mankind. His message binds man to *him*, to his spirit, and not to some cold law permanently threatening to become a trap.

And yet he is the most exacting of legislators, and insists on loyalty to the death and the involvement of one's whole being. "Enter through the narrow gate" (Matthew 7:13). It takes all one's will – in fact, that above all. "Not everyone who says to me, 'Lord, Lord,' will enter the kingdom of heaven, but only the one who does the will of my Father in heaven" (7:21).

When love does not correspond to the adhesion of our will to God, we must be wary. Only he who faithfully follows the Gospel will be like the man *who built his house on rock* (7:24). This is what gives the saints their security, their serenity in the storm and their peace in the midst of conflict.

24 November (Milad)

The centurion is an example of true humility (cf. Luke 7). He does not set store by his deeds (he had built a synagogue for the Jews), and he feels so strongly that he is unworthy to welcome Jesus to his house that, not only does he not come to petition Jesus himself, but, when he hears that Jesus is on his way, he sends someone to tell him not to trouble himself because he, the centurion, is unworthy. However, his humility is full of hope (two sides of the same sentiment), and he knows his request will be granted.

So, our humility must be rooted in an awareness of the infinite disparity between the creature and the Creator and in the sight of his marvellous design to make us his children, not in our wretchedness alone.

"Have mercy on us, O Lord."

The miracle of the resurrection of the widow's son in Nain (Luke 7:11–17) – an unsolicited miracle – tells us everything about the compassion of Jesus the man.

Jesus has to be considered as a man too, and a study of his humanity and his psychology is an extremely effective means of increasing our love for him.

The Last Day of the Liturgical Year

> Do you want peace? Seek to be last.
> Do you want humility? Seek to be last.
> Do you want love? Seek to be last.
> Do you want to find Jesus? Seek to be last.

28 November (Milad)

The Pharisee invites Jesus to his house to dine. A woman who has sinned comes into the room where they are eating and washes Jesus' feet (Luke 7:36 et seq.).

In love, who starts first? Man or God? Certainly God, but . . . he acts only when man loves. "Her sins, which were many, have been forgiven; hence she has shown great love." So is it she, the woman, who has the initiative? The person who has been forgiven much will love the more, so does God have it?

The mystery of the freedom of God and the freedom of man.

There is, however, one essential thing which must be stressed. Christianity is not made for a *happy medium*, a cautious life and rationed virtue. It is made for fanatics, for extremists, for totalitarians. What a lot there is to say on this topic!

The love of the Pharisee for Jesus – measured, without a kiss, without warmth – is set against the love of the sinning woman – overwhelming and genuine. The Pharisee's love certainly isn't the better, though it is the most common sort in the world among right-thinking and worthy men.

"How can this be, since I am a virgin?" (Luke 1:34 et seq.). This is the only protest Mary makes to the Angel's announcement of her consecration. The divine life within us is so great that it has to be put before any question of dignity, even that of being the mother of the Saviour. There are religious acts which have eternal value and which must not be put second to any human concern.

"Fiat mihi secundum verbum tuum."[5]

Reassured, Mary not only agrees, she even *welcomes* it now.

And the greatest possible event in history comes about: *the Incarnation of God*.

"My soul magnifies the Lord" (Luke 1:46). For the first time after the great event, Mary praises the Lord. Her song is a whole compendium of many Bibles, and reveals the spiritual nourishment of the Virgin. She calls God her saviour and above all she stresses the merciful nature of the gift. The only way to quell pride is to see everything as the fruit of divine mercy.

But the most striking thing is the feeling of great humility which pervades every word concerning "the lowliness of his servant".

Here is the profound meaning of every true relationship with God. Like an eagle, God swoops down on everything little, needy and humble. If there is something in man which restrains God, it is certainly pride, self-presumption and vanity.

This is the real lesson of the Magnificat.

When will the day come, O Lord, when I shall have no more problems? And what causes me so many problems if not pride and self-absorption? Oh, if I could only tear out this loathsome root growing in my heart, which is sick with that ancient poison! God who is humility, God who is giving, give me love. God who is forgiveness, give me mercy.

The afternoon hour of adoration

What a splendid answer to my prayer for tomorrow! What light!

But, O Lord, make the light shine steadily, otherwise my shadows will come back to plague me. Make this ardour last, or else my weakness will come out on top.

Humility?

Nurture Jesus' humility within you . . . humility, complete humility.

Jesus is the humility of God. To experience his feelings is to enter forever into the light and into truth and humility.

Jesus does nothing without the Father: you do the same. He refers everything to the Father: you do the same.

From his childhood to the cross, Jesus *depends* on the Father: that is humility. Do you depend on someone? That is your pride. Jesus has to begin. There he is in the desert, seeking the Father's will. What about you?

He has to choose the apostles, so he spends the night in prayer. And you? There is your pride, your presumption. He has to perform a miracle, and is almost afraid of gaining glory by it. And you? If you could, you would shout to the whole world: "Look at me!"

This morning, in front of the Blessed Host, you even had the diabolical nerve to imagine your beatification. However, you were checked by the long line of people knowing bad things about you and ready to testify against you.

What overweening pride! How shameful! God, have pity on me. Grant me the gift of your humility. Let me put an end to this farce intended to fool the world – strip me naked before you, as if I were about to die. Let this charred brand be rekindled. Is it still possible, O Lord? Can your omnipotence perform such a miracle?

God, have pity on your Carlo!

What exactly is humility, then? An awareness of one's sins, of one's lowliness? Thinking oneself the least of men, the most sinful? No, because in that case the Madonna, who had not sinned, could not have spoken as she did.

Humility is being certain of the congenital impossibility of our being saved, of our total incapacity to develop the divine part of our natures. Therefore it is the attitude of the spirit towards the divine. A desire to see, a desire to have the initiative to achieve divine ends in our own hands, is an attitude which is the very opposite of humility.

That is a realm in which we can do absolutely nothing, and humility has its roots there. The desire to define, to see clearly, to make decisions and to understand our own actions is tantamount to the destruction of humility in us.

Not for nothing does humility grow with faith; not for nothing is humility the spiritual aspect of hope. Only a humble person believes and hopes. In other words, it is the child who knows that he is totally dependent on the Father, but believes and is certain that nothing will happen to him, because he is in good hands.

The annunciation to Joseph

This is a good name for the passage in Matthew (1:18–25). This truly extraordinary Gospel text shines with the great light of Mary's and Joseph's faith. Joseph, faced with the incomprehensible fact of Mary's pregnancy, does not doubt her, but being unable to understand, he decides on a secret separation so that she will not be disgraced or compelled to give explanations. The Angel appears to him, and in announcing the great mystery, makes him the gift of a true, legal paternity: "You are to name him Jesus." Joseph stays silent, and obeys with a faith which is truly stupendous.

But why did Mary keep silent? Perhaps because, though living God's mystery, she didn't know how to talk about it. Exactly so: if we were

...d, we wouldn't be able to talk about it. Moreover, she is ... that if God, who had accomplished so many marvels, had ... known, he would have made the announcement himself ... olved the problem.

The whole thing, however, is perhaps one of the episodes in the Gospels where faith and hope are required of man, with maximum commitment and greatness of heart.

Mary and the soul

Advent; thoughts of Mary, encompassing all the millennia of waiting for the Saviour.

The Annunciation – Mary's faith – silence – for nine months she carries salvation alone. The divine mystery which clothes itself in Mary's spiritual humanity. Her role of mother. Her acceptance of the coming of Christ, and therefore her acceptance of my salvation. Union with Jesus on the cross – our co-redeemer, a new birth through her – mother of the Head, therefore mother of the Mystical Body of Christ.

Mary's discretion during her life. Her presence in the early Church, especially with John and his disciples. Co-redeemer – Mediator – Mother.

DECEMBER 1955

The Eve of the Immaculate Conception

Mary is a new creation. In view of the Incarnation and the merit accruing to her from the Passion of Jesus, God made Mary immaculate in Anne's womb.

She is the only healthy part of the body of humanity, which is rotten with sin, and she is the glorious beginning of the most wonderful manifestation of God's love.

The Feast of the Immaculate Conception

Mary is the masterpiece of creation. God's power acted twice for her. The first time was when he created the world; the second was when he decreed her immaculate conception in Anne's womb.

It was as if he had decreed a new dawn. Eve was the mother of all living people, Mary was to become the mother of all redeemed people. God's design, which had been frustrated by sin, now reappeared, more lovely and more sublime than ever.

Redemption was added to Incarnation.

Incarnation! God's sublime dream – the crowning of his love – marriage with his creature – he asked his creature to bear his Son!

What power does Mary have over God's heart? The power of a bride! With what love God alighted on her love, to make her fruitful!

What a sweet fruit was born from that love – Jesus, the Son, the true Son. The dream had come true – the secret hidden through the centuries – the holy family. It was the beginning of our deification.

Mary has extraordinary power. Everything is possible for this bride! And yet how silent she is before the Bridegroom! How little she feels herself to be! The abyss calls to the abyss! And all this was preordained. "The Lord created me at the beginning of his work, the first of his acts of long ago" (Proverbs 8:22).

Mary, sweet Mary, I love you.

Look down upon us.

You, who had no knowledge of the most horrible thing of all – sin – have pity on us sinners.

Help us to free ourselves from it.

Teach us to do that which was so easy for you: God's will.

Stand between us and Christ when we seem to be his enemies because we sin.

For love of you, he will forgive us again and always.

Mediatress for every grace!

Bridge over all abysses, since you joined the two most impossible extremes: the Creator and his creature.

Holy synthesis between the divine and the human.

You who made the invisible God visible, in the face of a man.

You were the one who made that face with your blood, in your peace.

Your womb is a heaven where God hid himself.

Your womb is a heaven from which God appeared to mankind.

You nourished God!

You clothed God!

God called you Mother!

Mary! Mary!

11–18 December

The last week of the novitiate. Oh, if only I knew how to live at least these last few days as the true novice of this great concept! I shall try, but it will be difficult.

Yesterday evening, as never before, I realized the possibility of considering Jesus as my tutor in loving the Father! Therefore, telling him one's defeats and failures in this field is a good thing. Little St Teresa used to do that by describing her errors down to the tiniest detail. The reality of the Mystical Body, and Jesus' action as its Head, has too little effect on me, one of its members.

Lord, before you I am like a starving man before bread, a thirsty man seeing a spring.

You are the sun, the earth, a mountain, a flower, light, strength and life.

Every created thing has something of you in it and teaches me how much I need you.

Every beautiful thing speaks to me of you, who are beauty. I wish I could suckle from you as a baby drinks milk; I would like to eat you up; I want to enter into you, become one with you, fuse myself with you.

Now I feel that this hunger and this thirst will last all my life, and the closer I come to you for your love's sake, the more I shall feel the need to eat you and drink you.

Oh, how real the Eucharist is! And how it satisfies our hunger!

Forgive me, O Lord, if I tell you that you practised a loving trick on us when you said: "I am the bread of life. Whoever comes to me will never be hungry" (John 6:35). You did it to draw us to you. But the hunger of your creatures for you can never be sated, until the day in which they will possess you for ever. And more than that . . . I cannot say.

I have started my retreat before taking my vows. I have made no plans or resolutions: they are useless!

This time, for the first time, I shall let the Lord decide everything. All I want to do is wait.

How tainted we are, O Lord! This poor machine you created with such perfection and wisdom is badly broken!

Who can repair it but you, O my Creator, O my Redeemer!

Sometimes I have the impression that the damage is so serious that – forgive me – not even you know how to set it right any more. It is like cloth which tears around the stitch; it is like a vintage car, losing parts all over the place.

Everything is possible for God – you said so – even getting a camel through the eye of a needle . . . and so . . .

God, my Doctor, treat me and I shall be cured; my Saviour, save me and I shall be saved.

Today and forever, until the end of my days.

That which is healed today goes back to being sick tomorrow, and so on, continually. Pull up the weed, and it grows again; wash the sore, and an hour later it is infected again.

It is a perpetual struggle against evil, with no quarter given, because evil ebbs and flows all the time.

This means one can't be confirmed in grace, and that means you are our *Redeemer forever*.

19 December
Five p.m.: a telephone call from Piero in Géryville.

20 December
Piero has arrived, chilled to the bone. Tomorrow he is going to begin the retreat with me.

21-24 December
Retreat at the Col.

Conclusions
My programme? Jesus. As far as I am concerned I have handed in my resignation. From now on he is in charge.

Commitment:

Always to choose the more painful of two things, the least pleasant, the least beautiful. Seek to be last.

"Everything is nothing, everything is nothing!" Milad exclaimed after a chapter, which was one of the most sincere I have ever attended.

One drop of Jesus' blood is all that's needed.

It is a question of faith and hope. The mystery of a God who takes flesh for me, who dies for me, is so immense that the foulest heap of sin immediately takes fire from God's love.

What comfort there is in these words! How desperately I want to be reborn in Jesus tonight, to be his forever, his slave, his servant, entirely at his command, in total surrender to him. Mary, help me to be reborn!

Christmas Day

I am a Little Brother. I buried the old Professor in the caves of the Col at Géryville. Now I am beginning a new life.

The most important feature of my spiritual life is my total renunciation of guiding myself, of concerning myself with and analyzing the procedures of my Christian life. I have relinquished all this to God.

From now on I want to keep my eyes on him, and him alone. He will take care of me. My act of faith must be complete and without second thoughts. Gifts have come for me too, but . . . I am afraid to open the parcel. We shall see in the days to come.

Works! Houses without the Father, churches without God, kitchens without a fire, bedrooms without love.

Method! Work makes you lose weight, poverty sets you free. So, having become light, you get used to praying. The least that can happen to you is that you take flight. And the desert which stretches away before you – awe-inspiring, silent, infinite – beckons you to seek its heart, where you will be alone, alone with your God.

Working priests and Little Brothers: a pastoral presence and a religious presence.

Appendices

An Address by Professor Carlo Carretto

In my opinion this is the best Central Council of the last six years. I think very few people can have the joy of not bearing a load of responsibility on their shoulders, unlike myself. Over the past three days I have thoroughly enjoyed myself!

Joking apart, however, I thank you all. I especially want to thank Mario, who was so good as to invite me here to greet you. My presence here is not intended to ensure the peaceful continuity of our movement; that is guaranteed in that our projects are eminently practical, springing as they do from souls dedicated to the apostolate and to contact with other people, rather than from pseudo-intellectual brains. The plans which we of the Gioventu have made can always be re-examined from top to bottom in order to clarify our position and to see whether there is scope for improvement or a greater degree of involvement, but in the end, ours is the line to follow.

My thanks for this invitation must be taken as a thank-you, not for the continuity, but for your display of affection – which, I assure you, is a great comfort to me.

I don't know if you have ever felt how sharp the pangs of remorse can be: remorse for neglecting to do, or not being able to do, something which ought to have been done. There are difficult moments in the life of the soul; moments that I have personally been through lately. During the month I spent in a retreat in Jesus' homeland, I particularly suffered from that feeling of remorse, and if I were to find myself face to face with God, I would not have the courage to say: "I was the Director of the GIAC." Instead, your affection and warmth console me, and put a little salve on this wound which every man has to bear through life, and which, I believe, helps us to love the Lord more.

What can I tell you as I greet you on this occasion? Listen, I have been far away, as you all know; I have been all over the world and can assure you that the way of the Gioventù, and the idea behind Catholic Action, are universally relevant. Therefore it comes spontaneously from the soul to advise any apostle, priest or bishop to follow the guidelines of Catholic Action in setting up an organization. Thus they can be sure that what has been done is right, reasonable, obeys the dictates of God's will and has already produced results.

The continents I have visited on my travels have left me with the clear impression that if Catholic Action were applied thoroughly in the missions, and if their work were carried out by the methods of our Organization, things would go far better in the future.

So much for the central idea. What about method? During those forty days in the East I thought a great deal about it. In the period between the last Council chaired by me and the first one chaired by Mario, if I had been asked to say something to you about method, I wouldn't have known what to say. I am totally convinced that it is not a question of method! Method is necessary – I don't mean to undervalue it – but that is not where the real problem lies. Today I think I would found an association in a country with only ten souls, all of different ages and callings, including a little boy and an old man. I would not worry about methodology!

At the end of everything, the sum of all my thinking is that I have discovered that Christianity is not to be found only there, though it is also there. One sunny day, I visited the site of the temptation of Jesus, high up over the great valley where he could see the whole history of his people spread out. I stood on the mount of temptation, thinking and meditating on my work; I thought of the temptations of the apostolate. What tricks had been played on us – on me? And this is what came to me: when the devil is dealing with an executive of Catholic Action, he is wasting his time if he tries to invent ways of making him back down, or raise doubts about his faith which would make him leave Catholic Youth and the Church. Instead of tempting us by pulling us back, he does so by hurrying us forwards along the path we are best cut out for. Many temptations passed before my eyes, from the joy of hearing people talk about social programmes, to the pleasure of listening to a sermon, until I came to my personal temptations: organizing things, for example, pressing ahead without stopping, and believing in those things as if the salvation of souls depended on them; so it turns into a never-ending race which eventually becomes a torment.

I recall the Central Council which gave me most joy: the one on social problems. It is possible to become fanatical about social problems, and to weep on hearing about a little boy who goes home and has no money for milk, and yet not be able to act in love and charity on behalf of one's fellow beings. So, justice degenerates into a perfect knowledge of the case, allied with a heart more gelid than a block of ice. Perhaps we have forgotten the simplicity of the child crying before the altar of the Madonna.

The same is true for the question of Christian lore, which has turned Christianity into a complicated affair, and we forget that it is a simple act: "Do this and you will live."

I am not interested in either specialization or unity. What Jesus says – and it's true – is this: "Not by the will of man, but by the will of God I was born." Christianity is always this mysterious birth, which God effects in the soul by random or complex means.

Therefore, if I were to tell you something, as I greet you and thank you for the great affection you have shown me, this is what it would be: these things have to be done, but once they are done we must not think that is all; or else, let us make sure they have that extra something, which is closeness to God. It is possible to be a good organizer and yet be unworthy to carry a GIAC membership card in one's pocket.

To the younger people present, I wish a long series of Central Councils, here in Rome or wherever the Director may decide.

To my dear Mario, who carries such a heavy burden – I can sympathize with him more than anybody because I have shared his experience – I wish that the Madonna, whom he loves so dearly, may support him in this struggle, and may he be a better brother to you than I ever managed to be.

(From the proceedings of the GIAC Central Council held in Rome at the Villa "Il Maestro" from 31 January to 2 February 1953, presided over by Mario Rossi.)

APPENDIX 2

Charles de Foucauld
Founder of the Little Brothers of Jesus

All his days Charles de Foucauld[1] was inspired by the idea of gathering "brothers" together, to share his way of life with him. This idea came to him in his third year in a Trappist monastery, and it stayed with him until his death . . . He never lost hope, despite Abbot Huvelin's initial opposition, endless disappointments and the long, lonely wait. Gentle and strong, he humbly accepted the apparent failure of his dearest wish as the result of his unworthiness. And yet, he knew very well that this was what he had been sent for. His notes, letters and rules reveal that he often created ideal "Fraternities" in his imagination. He even made minutely detailed plans for them, and envisaged them already scattered throughout the world, like beacons radiating faith and love, carrying "fire to the whole world" . . .

And yet, he was not fated to see his "Little Brothers" while he was alive. He had to shed his blood, and he was alone when he was struck down on the threshold of his Ahaggar hermitage.

It seemed as if nothing of Brother Charles' work was to survive, and yet, little by little, the seed took root and grew. The hermit of the Sahara's message of evangelical love moved many souls throughout the world, and disciples began to arrive . . .

The case of Father de Foucauld as the founder of an order is probably unique in the history of the Church: a founder who founded nothing while he was alive, but a *de facto* hermit who, living in solitude and lacking any experience of community life, worked out detailed constitutions and rules for a congregation of men and a congregation of women. More than fifteen years after his death those plans were made into a reality . . . If he is the founder, he can't be one in the sense usually understood by the Church.[2] The difficulties are immediately apparent: on the one hand there are numerous books of rules, not only different to each other, but in places apparently contradictory; on the other hand is the absolute, undeniable fact of an ardent life which overwhelms any written word rising above it in its complex and yet simple unity. Yet the founder is not here to explain his thoughts or to help us to interpret a rule which is often meticulous and unbending in the extreme. And yet, through all these writings there shone an intense glow of faith and evangelical love which uplifted souls and propelled them inexorably towards the fulfilment of an ideal, which could only be lived once the details had been settled.

The Fraternity of El-Abiodh-Sidi-Cheikh

It is very hard to fit Father de Foucauld's life, which was dedicated to the service of God and mankind, into any of the usual categories: monk, missionary, active, contemplative . . . Consequently "it is not possible straight away to understand the profound unity of this extraordinary life which has so many extremely rich, and sometimes apparently contradictory, sides to it. Nor can one identify the central and fruitful idea (often obscured and made almost intractable by the excessively detailed or too-personal rules) behind his successive projects for foundations. This identification was only made possible by long experience and considerable reflection on the message contained in the writings and life of Father de Foucauld . . . The slowness, the hesitations and, at times, the discrepancies between the various attempts to set up foundations over the past twenty years or so, will be understood and excused." (Written in 1946.)

To begin with, isolated attempts to imitate his life were made by generous priests in southern Tunisia and in Morocco. But it was only in 1933 that the religious congregations came into being: the "Little Brothers" and the "Little Sisters of the Sacred Heart". They were followed in 1936 by the "Little Sisters of Jesus".

"Near the small oasis of El-Abiodh-Sidi-Cheikh in the Sahara in southern Oran, the first foundation of the Little Brothers was established, after Cardinal Verdier, Archbishop of Paris, had invested the first five brothers in the Basilica of Montmartre on Friday 8 September 1933."

The founding of El-Abiodh did not occur from one day to the next: it evolved from a combination of individual experiences, lucky encounters and joint decisions . . . In 1944 Brother René Voillaume described the genesis of this foundation in some hitherto unpublished notes. Here are some extracts from them:

"In 1926 the aspirations of many of us, which had been more or less unfocused up till then, began to acquire form and clarity. A combination of fortunate circumstances had brought us together, so that a foundation began to look like a distinct possibility. At the time we were all theology students at the big seminary of Issy-les-Moulineaux, and the foundation could not be created immediately. We had read the life of Father de Foucauld by René Bazin, followed by the *Spiritual Writings*, and a keen desire to emulate the hermit of Béni Abbès awoke in us. It looked as if the necessary requirements were all there for a monastic and missionary life, centred around the adoration of the Eucharist . . . But this all remained a hazy notion; we had no experience and were unable to imagine the problems that would arise without a profound knowledge of the plans and spirit of Father de Foucauld. We could not have described the exact nature of the foundation we were dreaming of.

"During the year 1927-1928, in the seminary at Issy, one of us managed – I have no idea how – to get hold of the little book written by Father de Foucauld himself, which contained the rule of 1899. We were filled with enthusiasm, and showed the manuscript to M. Boisard, Father Superior of the community for theological studies. After reading it he returned it to us with his verdict: it was infinitely touching and edifying, but absolutely impracticable. The rule had been written 'for a community of angels, not men'. I'm not sure we fully believed him! Still, we did realize that changes needed to be made.

"The following year two of us met M. Massignon, who we admired because he had been the friend and confidant of Father de Foucauld and his spiritual heir . . . One of us was chosen, by common accord, to be 'the provisional leader of the movement' – that was the title we chose – and it was decided that after his ordination to the priesthood in June 1929, he would go to Rome to study theology for two years.

Thus he had the chance to put his ideas to a few prominent people in Rome, including Mgr d'Herbigny, who viewed the project very favourably and even spoke of it, in the course of two meetings, to His Holiness Pope Pius XI, who gave us his blessing and his support . . .

"On being told, they (the White Fathers) seemed to be in favour of the idea, but they heavily stressed the fact that Father de Foucauld had only intended to found an exclusively contemplative congregation, and that, against his will, he had been persuaded to work in the missionary apostolate; his true ideal was clearly embodied in the 1899 rule. And so we were compelled to examine the rule again from start to finish.

"In the autumn of 1931, one of us went to the Sahara and got in touch with Mgr Nouet, who welcomed us to his (apostolic) Prefecture. On the advice of the Superiors of the White Fathers, we enrolled in a two-year course offered by the Institute of Arabic Letters in Tunis (1931–1932); two of us in the first year and four of us in the second. Meanwhile many of us got in touch with the Carthusians of Montrieux, which enabled the latter to get to know the 1899 rule and to make some wise comments on the subject.

"In the summer of 1932, we all gathered in a retreat at the Trappist Monastery of Notre Dame des Dombes. There, the general outline of our project was set out in a series of instructions, by the person who had been elected provisional superior. A number of points appeared to be fairly clear already; in particular, Eucharistic adoration, emulation of the life of Nazareth and our intention of adapting to the local culture, from the monastic point of view, above all: we wanted to offer a genuine form of contemplative life to native vocations, suited to their mentality and their abilities. At first sight, it appeared that this objective of the Fraternities in the field had been completely understood, thanks to papal directives on the subject, and to the needs of the missions . . ."

"A brief note on the order created by Father de Foucauld and called by him the 'Little Brothers of the Sacred Heart':[3]

"Now Providence appears to favour the project by inspiring a number of priests with this vocation, and they have been quietly preparing themselves for several years, with the approval of their bishops . . .

"Changes will have to be made in the constitutions left us by Father de Foucauld, since the rule, though written for a community, was never actually tried out in communal conditions and, moreover, was elaborated by an exceptionally gifted man of great physical strength and moral character.

"Despite modifications to the letter of the rule, its spirit will stay exactly the same. It is summed up briefly in Clause 1 of the Constitutions (of Father de Foucauld): 'The Little Brothers of the Sacred Heart of Jesus have the special vocation, first of all to imitate Our Lord Jesus Christ in his hidden life in Nazareth, then to observe perpetual adoration of the displayed Holy Sacrament, and to live in the lands of their mission.'

"Therefore it is to be a contemplative order devoted exclusively to missionary work in the field, in all countries without exception, with a special spirit of humility, poverty, charity and devotion to Jesus in the Eucharist.

"Its principal aim is to take the graces of conversion to those countries where the monasteries are to be set up; prayer and penitence will have a purely apostolic function. The monastic ideal will be combined with self-abnegation and humble and loving surrender to God, in order to convert souls, through grace above all. A profound and daily communion with Jesus in the Eucharist is observed, to which the Little Brothers owe particular devotion.

"In those countries where evangelization is more advanced and where there are already a large number of conversions, the task of the Little Brothers will also be to take monastic life to the missions, by founding monasteries with a rule suited to the climate, the local culture and way of life.

"If God wills, the first foundation will take place next October in the Atlas Mountains of Southern Algeria, in the Apostolic Prefecture of Ghardaia . . .

"This choice is justified by the fact that, apart from the tactful and fraternal support given by the White Fathers to our fledgling enterprise, the majority of the Little Brothers have vocations which are clearly orientated towards the conversion of Muslims."

The final preparations for the foundation were made during 1933. Another journey to the Sahara led to a final choice of location: El-Abiodh-Sidi-Cheikh. All those who were due to leave met at a retreat in Viry-Chatillon, in the Paris suburbs, at the beginning of September; Mgr Roland Gosselin, Bishop of Versailles, was to have presided over their investiture at the end of the retreat. "But on his advice, we got in touch with Cardinal Verdier, asking that the ceremony be held in Montmartre, and he agreed. It was all to take place in great secrecy, and in private. Without our knowledge, however, the cardinal was persuaded to whip up a lot of publicity, and on the day we found ourselves in the presence of a great crowd in the upper church; the ceremony took place under the glare of lights (reporters' flashes). We still find the memory a painful one."

And so the "founding" of the Fraternity was written up in the press. For example, it appeared on the front page of La Croix with an impressive headline:

"Before disappearing into the depths of the Sahara, the Little Brothers of the Sacred Heart take the habit in Montmartre.

"It was known that before his death Father de Foucauld had planned three foundations to carry on his work: the Charles de Foucauld Association, a Congregation of Little Sisters of the Sacred Heart and a Congregation of Little Brothers of the Sacred Heart.

"The Charles de Foucauld Association has been in existence for some time and is run efficiently by its scrupulous and active Vicar-General, Dupin. The Congregation of the Little Sisters is to be founded soon. On Friday afternoon the first five Little Brothers received their habit in the Basilica of Sacré Coeur in Montmartre . . .

"At 3 p.m. His Eminence Cardinal Verdier entered the pulpit. The choir was already packed with a large number of priests and religious including Mgr Boucher, Vicar-General Dupin and M. Weber, Father Superior of the Issy Seminary; Father Duriaux OP, who held a retreat for the future missionaries; Canon Richaud, Ecclesiastic Assistant of Catholic Action; Canon Lieutier; Abbot Bordet, Deputy Chaplain-

General of the JOC. In the front rows of the assembly with the families of the missionaries, were M. Laurain, Secretary of the above Association, devised by Father de Foucauld himself; M. Massignon, Professor at the Collège de France; André Hesse, Secretary General of the JOC, who was there, as was Abbot Bordet, because three of the little Brothers had been JOC chaplains.

"After the congregation had sung the Magnificat, His Emminence Cardinal Verdier began to speak. With deep emotion, the Archbishop of Paris hailed the birth of a great enterprise, one which Father de Foucauld had longed and planned for. He knew that it would not happen during his lifetime, and that it was God's will that he should die so that it could become a reality. What enterprise is this? The religious conquest of the Muslim peoples, for whose salvation Charles de Foucauld had shed his blood. Like him, the apostles about to set out intend to convert them through prayer, charity and by offering the example of a rigorous and hard-working life. 'May God bless you! May he transform your hearts . . . and inform them with a new flame of love and lead you to give yourselves without stinting, to the peoples you are travelling to live amongst.'

"In conclusion, the speaker evoked the memory of St Ignatius and his disciples, who gathered together on the hill of Montmartre before separating to accomplish the magnificent work of the Company of Jesus, and he wished the new Order an equally successful future . . .

"Then, having taken off their old habits, the Little Brothers appeared in their religious habits – a long white robe with a hood, a leather belt and a white scapular with a red heart below a cross, also red; the clothes in which Father de Foucauld is usually depicted. In turn, the Reverend Fathers Voillaume (Father Superior of the new community), Bouchet, Gorrée, Champenois and Gerin, all ex-students of St Sulpice, climbed the steps of the choir and went to place their hands in those of the Cardinal, to pronounce their first profession and receive his embrace. After this there was the traditional Friday procession which was followed by Cardinal Verdier since the Little Brothers walked before Jesus in the Eucharist. The blessing of the Holy Sacrament was sung. Before the Tantum Ergo, the future missionaries went back to the choir; this time they went to the altar, where they read a very simple and moving act of consecration to the Sacred Heart in French and then Arabic, accompanied by a piercingly sweet song to the Virgin, also in Arabic . . .

"That evening they left Paris for El-Abiodh-Sidi-Cheikh, in southern Oran, where they will be living in the middle of the desert, more than 120 kilometres away from any French soil."

Built in Saharan style around an old military *bordij*, the Fraternity stands at the edge of the desert. The *bordij* was built after the great revolt of Bou-Amama,[4] near the three *ksour* (villages) which make up El-Abiodh. This is the religious centre of the Oulad Sidi-Cheikh tribe, because it is the burial site of Sidi-Cheikh, a famous Muslim holy man who died in the seventeenth century and who built up an active following stretching from the northern Sahara as far as Morocco.

"In October 1933, a few days after our investiture, the provisional rule came into force. (This rule, observed by the first brothers, followed the projected rule written by Father de Foucauld in 1899; later it was modified and new details were added.) For us this text held the essence of Father de Foucauld's thought, and I don't think that in those days we had quite realized that his thought was more extensive, gentler and more complex, surpassing by far the bounds of this rule . . . At the same time we felt the influence, accumulated over the centuries, of the Carthusians and the Carmelite way of life. We had not yet penetrated deeply enough into Father de Foucauld's thought to be able to assimilate this outside contribution, which was so valid in many ways. Could it have been otherwise, given that we ourselves had no experience, and were unable to look beyond the guidance and the advice of the old order? I think not.

"Indeed, the difference between us and the 1899 rule became so obvious, that the latter became an impediment . . . (But) it is partly to the Carthusians that we owe the solidity of our contemplative life, our deep commitment to our 'ministry of prayer', and that true solitude in which the final stripping of the soul as it goes to meet its God takes place . . .

"These outside influences did not stop the Fraternity from preserving its original character and developing along its chosen lines. Its most salient features were above all its adaptation to local cultures – this was certainly the aspect which struck visitors to El-Abiodh most forcibly – and Eucharistic adoration."

On 19 March 1936, the feast-day of St Joseph, Mgr Nouet, Apostolic Prefect of the Sahara, conferred the status of diocesan congregation on the Fraternity, after the authorities in Rome had examined the constitutions and approved them *ad experimentum* for a period of five years.

The moment of expansion

"The first Fraternity was built in Islamic territory over twelve years ago now. Its spirit matured in the silence of the desert. Now Providence seems to be telling us that given the circumstances, the time has come to branch out. The building of a second foundation in the mountains among the Berbers, begun a year ago, and plans for a Fraternity in the industrial, lapsed Christian centre of France, are coming along well.

"Requests from Vicars-Apostolic for the foundation of Fraternities constantly draw our attention to other countries outside the Islamic world in need of missions. These new prospects are matched by the growing number of applications for admission to our Fraternities."

Written in 1946, these lines refer to the propitious events which had fundamental consequences for the Fraternity, at least as regards its development and its future. It is not possible to go into them in any detail here. However, it can be said that they occurred on two levels:

"In the light of experience, and with a greater knowledge of the ideal embodied by Father de Foucauld, there was a shift of focus within the foundation, in the sense that its life concentrated more on working for a living and on closer contact with the local people: smaller Fraternities evolved, with not more than three to five brothers, and with humbler accommodation. At this point foundations began to spread to other towns and countries."

This evolution was the outcome of the seeking, the experiments and the trials caused by the "considerable difference between our life" and the "1899 rule" of de Foucauld, mentioned by Brother René

Voillaume in his notes on the history and founding of El-Abiodh. In his conclusion he wrote: "What has been missing is a strong enough presence of the soul and spirit of Father de Foucauld – a certain atmosphere of poverty and work – a more profound commitment to the mystery of the hidden life of Nazareth."

On the other hand, during the Second World War and the immediate post-war years, "France, the new missionary field" experienced its well-known apostolic revival. The brothers of El Abiodh discovered it just when normal contacts were re-established with Algeria. How could they fail to recognize the confirmation of their vocations in this situation, or the need to stay on in circumstances where generosity, a degree of risk and, at times, of ambiguity were combined! This is confirmed in the following article, published "prematurely" at the end of 1946. The first Fraternity in the de-Christianized industrial regions had been intended to be discreet; the rapid growth of the project, however, made it newsworthy.

"With every passing day Father de Foucauld emerges more clearly as the bearer of a spiritual message which is eminently relevant for our times . . . But there is more: Charles de Foucauld also received the mission to awaken a new form of religious life within the Church . . .

"The vocation of Brother Charles and the Little Brothers essentially consists of imitating, for love, Jesus when he lived and worked in Nazareth, by leading as he did, a contemplative life of poverty and work amidst other people, and having a simple and close relationship with them. This call to imitate the life of Nazareth is the main characteristic of Charles de Foucauld's vocation. But it was only gradually, as his life unfolded, that he came to perceive all the strands of his ideal: he lived them, one might say, before he thought of them, and one step at a time he achieved complete and admirable fulfilment during the years he spent in Tamanrasset.

"To imitate the life of Jesus in Nazareth: until then, it seems to us, this ideal of life primarily evoked the hidden virtues of humility, poverty, prayer and humble and silent work: and that was how the majority of religious Congregations consecrated to prayer or to the apostolate had interpreted it. This was still the aspect which initially struck the newly converted Charles de Foucauld, and which led him first to the Trappists and then to Nazareth, where he intended to become a lowly servant forgotten by all, and to disappear from sight, so he could be alone with Jesus in the tabernacle and in his intimate daily life in the Holy Family with Mary and Joseph.

"The rule of the Little Brothers of the Sacred Heart, written in 1899 at the end of those two years of meditation and solitude, is totally permeated with this mystical concept. It shows us an ideal Fraternity, secluded and centred around the Holy Sacrament which is its soul, just as Jesus was the soul of the house in Nazareth. Though they have an extremely personal and original slant to them, these plans for a congregation did not propose a life so very different from that of the Trappists. The influence of the Cistercian rule, which the religious soul of Brother Alberic evolved over the years, is obvious.

"Charles de Foucauld's stay in the Holy Land was a novitiate and a time of waiting. As he listened to the promptings of his true vocation, he was drawn towards the priesthood. Gradually he discovered another aspect of the life of Nazareth: Jesus had lived there as one of the villagers, and led the simplest of existences with his work, his family and his neighbours. Influenced by the growth of an immense, tender and fraternal love for people, Charles de Foucauld found this new side to his vocation in his day-to-day relationships with those around him, first in Béni Abbès and then in Tamanrasset. The simplicity with which he lived among the peoples of the Ahaggar Mountains, as "one of them", is common knowledge . . .

"For many years now the Fraternities have been striving to fulfil this ideal. This experience has served to clarify the nature of our contemplative life, the sort of contact to have with the local people in order to conform to the spirit of Nazareth and, finally, the way to organize a life of real poverty based on work.

"The life of the Little Brothers is still contemplative, not only because it focuses entirely on the Eucharist and the adoration of the Holy Sacrament, but also because it excludes all the usual outside activities of sacerdotal ministry in the strict sense of the word (parish or mission, Catholic Action chaplaincy, the ministry of predication and so on) and even all teaching or charitable activities, whatever they might be.

"The Eucharist, then, lies at the heart of the Little Brothers' spirituality; they must surrender to it completely in a spirit of love and adoration, so that God is free to shape them to the mystery of Eucharistic oblation. Through prayer and their daily life, they perpetuate the redeeming immolation of Christ in the Holy Sacrifice, which is the focal point of their day. This Eucharistic life also finds expression and sustenance in the communal recitation of the Office, and the adoration of the Holy Sacrament. An attitude of this sort is usually perfected by the spiritual acceptance of total immolation of self for the salvation of souls: for this reason the Little Brothers add the vow of self-abnegation to the three vows of poverty, chastity and obedience. Self-abnegation is their intention in the total sacrifice of their perpetual profession.

"The Little Brothers also find in the Holy Eucharist the source of that all-encompassing love for mankind which leads them to serve their brothers and share the burden of their crosses and day-to-day problems, as their father, Charles de Foucauld, knew how to do so well. It is particularly well known how he unhesitatingly accepted going without the actual presence of Jesus in the tabernacle, which at the time was the inevitable consequence of living in the Ahaggar region. Did not this supreme divestment in the expression of his devotion to the Holy Sacrament lead to an even greater plenitude in the Eucharistic life?

"The kind of work that a Little Brother must do as part of his commitment to other people in order to live like Jesus, obviously depends on circumstances in the individual missions. This approach must be fairly elastic, while taking great care to avoid aberrations which would compromise the whole mission of the Fraternities. These contacts must help the Little Brothers in their contemplative life to stay in touch with human suffering, daily tribulations and distress, especially in today's world. By living a life of poverty and hard work, they aspire to share the lives of working people, and in this knowledge born of experience they find the secret of giving themselves more completely and an incentive for their life of prayer.

"Mingling with other people, like yeast in dough, the Fraternities must radiate brotherly love and evangelical virtues. The Little Brothers are simply at the service of all through reciprocal aid, friendship, giving advice and making and receiving friendly visits. But their activities must always keep within the same bounds as those of a family living in the same place. As we have stressed, the problem to avoid – one might even say the temptation to resist – is that of organizing projects and services. The Little Brothers may not plan or take charge of them, but they are allowed to take part to the extent that a family might. Their mission is to bear witness on a more contemplative level. If they want their religious life in its outward appearances and its daily round (housing, clothes and working methods) to be as similar as possible to that of those around them, it is precisely so as to preserve their testimony of love and evangelical poverty. Their intention is to translate and illustrate Christ's message in terms of simple language and ordinary gestures. The Little Brothers aspire to love without expecting anything in return, and no self-seeking motive – however exalted and sublime – must be allowed to influence their lives. They live for the love of Jesus, for him alone, and if they love their fellow beings passionately, they do so in the name of 'the Lord's commandment'.

"Their way of life makes no claim to be a new form of apostolate and missionary conquest in the usual sense. If any of the Fraternities should become a shining testimony to Christ, it must not be sought as an end in itself.

"The organization of a life of poverty based on labour then, is one of the most important goals that the Fraternities must aim for. In order to present an effective testimony of poverty to the world, religious life must be able to prove itself completely without possessions or income, and be unafraid to shoulder the insecurity, the difficulties and the drawbacks of working for a wage. Whatever happens, Father de Foucauld's followers have to try to achieve this ideal: we are absolutely convinced, however, that after an inevitable period of adjustment and feeling their way, the Fraternities will manage to become self-supporting, thanks to the work of the Brothers . . .

"Within the Fraternities, work is to be seen as an instrument of asceticism and self-denial in its own right, and only by paying this price will they succeed in giving a contemporary image to religious poverty which will make it recognizable to all who seek for Christ. Especially among the pagan working classes, who at present seem more susceptible to an example taken from life than to a sermon, it will be the best way to communicate Christ silently.

"All we have said so far implies that the Fraternities will soon be found in industrial areas as well as in Islamic countries; a thing which will surprise the many readers for whom Father de Foucauld's ideal is indissolubly bound to the Sahara and to the Tuareg, or at least to the Muslim Arab peoples. And yet, there is nothing more misleading than to confine Father de Foucauld's ideal to this. He consecrated himself entirely to the peoples of the Sahara because the gift of self, to be complete, must be specific in practical terms, and also because fortuitous circumstances had prepared him personally for contact with these peoples. But, when he speaks of the Fraternities, his intention becomes universal . . . And if he reveals a preference, it is simply for the poorer, more neglected, more run-down areas. Otherwise, who would take care of our de-Christianized working-class masses? . . .

"The first working Fraternity in France is in the planning stage at present and will be opened in 1947. The experiment will involve finding outside employment. The Little Brothers will work in simplicity like the poor, to earn a living at jobs which may differ greatly from each other, each according to his abilities. The only condition required of the chosen job is that it be compatible with a true spiritual life.

"Since this first attempt at religious life is still on the drawing-board, we would have preferred not to mention it. We believe that in this case only facts should count. But we have already been asked so many questions about it that we felt it was necessary at least to describe the spirit in which this project will be carried out. It is also right to offer, as of now, the chance of guidance to those whom God may call. We know that the enterprise will be a tricky one: many problems will arise which we will only be able to solve with experience. The Little Brothers will embark on their first working Fraternity in a spirit of simple trust, with absolute faith in Father de Foucauld's ideal and, above all, in the promises and teachings of Jesus in the Gospel . . ."

Some major landmarks
It will be some time before an overall picture of the Fraternities and the Brothers as they are today becomes clear.

The situation still bears the signs of the multiplication and spread of the Fraternities during the fifties; more than a third of today's Fraternities were founded before 1960. From 1950 onwards, in fact, in difficult circumstances, the Brothers and also the Little Sisters of Jesus, with whom strong ties have been forged, went *Dal Sahara al mondo intero*.[5]

Thus, on the twentieth anniversary of the founding of the Order, Brother René Voillaume was able to write to the Brothers: "That the Lord supervised everything seems so obvious to me that above all, a feeling of total dependence on him must predominate in our souls . . . We really had no idea, when we arrived in El-Abiodh on 6 October 1933, where God was leading us. Only God knows the measure of our faith, but I believe Jesus took our weakness and our willingness into account, and arranged things so that our failings should not impede the accomplishment of his will. I know that this year will make its mark on the development and the spirit of the Fraternities, making them more universal and more faithful to the will of God." (Part of a letter from Katara, Urundi, 8 September 1953.)

From 1960 onwards the *News-sheet*, initially sporadic and cyclostyled for the families of the Brothers, came out every quarter and gave an idea of what was happening in the Fraternities.

As the Order expanded, the need was felt to compile a book of personal experiences, which would reveal the spiritual essence of the Fraternities. *Come loro* ["Like them"] contains the most important letters and talks addressed to the Little Brothers by the Prior over the period (1946-50) during which the Fraternity took shape and its spirit was established. On the front page of the first cyclostyled copy is the recently painted fresco in the refectory at El-Abiodh: it depicts Jesus on the cross, offering salvation to all – Muslims and workers. Brother Charles is shown dying at the foot of the cross and being "served" by his Little Brothers.

The book was published in 1950 in the "Incontri" series. The first book in the series was *Francia, paese di missione*, and this was subsequently translated and reissued. In the preface, Mgr de Provenchères rejoiced that these writings were being made available to the public, since they were "addressed to all those who thirst to love and serve the Lord", and because "there is a grace for the modern world in the message of Brother Charles of Jesus". Only God knows how many Christians and non-Christians drew light and strength from the book. Today it is difficult to gauge the impact of this publication. For interest's sake, this is what a critic wrote about it:

"One's first impression on reading this book is of exceptional spiritual health and great human and supernatural equilibrium . . . Just as one distrusts those spiritual types who keep no rein on their imagination, their feelings or the impression they give others, here one is reassured by the solid common sense, the accurate historical and canonical information, the profound theological thought and – despite appearances – by the respect throughout for the soundest and most genuine things handed down by tradition.

"The complete novelty of the work in question leaves one with no sense of discomfort. And this is significant. Innovators generally arouse feelings of unease or confusion, or at any rate, make the people around them feel uncomfortable. Here it is quite the opposite. There is so much clarity, openness and evangelical feeling that critics are disarmed right from the start; Father Voillaume is entirely lucid. Read his talk on Nazareth, the one on the form of religious life, the one on the contemplative life of the Fraternity, the one on asceticism in the Fraternities . . . He is aware that the life he directs under the auspices of Father de Foucauld cannot be fitted into any of the existing categories . . . this throws the canonist into confusion: his classifications are no longer applicable. And those with a logical turn of mind ought to feel uncomfortable too, on reading these pages. But not so. There is such sure diagnosis, such an affinity with the realities of life in the major industrial centres where there is a painful lack of evangelical witness, that one finishes the book with a feeling of serenity and faith. One finds oneself agreeing with Gamaliel, that if this work is not of God it will fail on its own (cf. Acts 5:38–39). Since, exacting and severe, it imposes this spiritual harmony on itself and testifies to it, it can only be Heaven's solution to the malaise in the circles it was written for . . .

"This is one of those books which, once read, becomes a focus for meditation and an aid to prayer.

"And for this we must thank the Lord."

On 15 August 1957, the Feast of the Assumption, Mgr Mercier, Bishop of Laghouat (Sahara), "given the unanimous approval of the twenty-seven Ordinaries (bishops) of the Fraternities scattered throughout the world" and "in his own name" gave "final approval to the Constitutions of the Congregation of the Little Brothers of Jesus".

Eleven years later the Fraternity acceded to papal law; in other words, the Church, in response to petitions from the most exalted ranks, pronounced on the authenticity of the Fraternity's "charism". On 13 June 1968, the Feast of the Most Holy Body and Blood of Christ, the Holy See recognized that:

"The institution called the Little Brothers of Jesus . . . following the example of Nazareth . . . has as its aim and its fulfilment, a contemplative life peculiar to it, the adoration of Christ in the Holy Sacrament, the practice of evangelical poverty, manual labour, and a genuine identification with the social condition of the very poor . . ."

At the same time the Holy See approved the modified Constitutions, and explicitly mentioned some articles, such as Article 3, where the Church confirms the Brothers in their mission to "dedicate themselves to the contemplative life while sharing, like Jesus in Nazareth, the life of those who have neither a name nor influence in the world. The life of Nazareth, consisting of poverty, concealment and hard work, is not merely the framework but also the stuff of their religious life."

APPENDIX 3

The Testimony of Arturo Paoli

It was getting on towards mid-November 1954 in El-Abiodh, the white village lying on the edge of the desert, when I received a phone call from Carlo Carretto to say that he was coming to begin his novitiate.

It was the only call I got in the thirteen months of my novitiate and it was a big, and pleasant, surprise. I had met Carlo in Rome several times after he resigned as Director of the GIAC, and we had shared the burden and the bitterness of the difficult period we were going through, without wondering what the future had in store for us. I was still assistant to Rossi, the new Director, with whom we made an effort to row against the current, well aware that we wouldn't be able to move the boat very far. I can testify on behalf of these two friends that our dearly beloved Friend has called to feast with him in heaven, that neither one was concerned for himself, his career or his future, but only for the Church, Gioventù and for the Kingdom of God.

Then Carlo told me of a sudden decision he had taken, a light which had dazzled him on 4 November, the feast-day of St Charles. It can't be described as a conversion, as in the case of Brother Charles de Foucauld, but I believe that Carlo Carretto, in the period between leaving the directorate and November 1954, had a very similar experience to that of Brother Charles: that same sense of uselessness, that waiting for new opportunities, the hope and frustration, that feeling of emptiness, which are often the signs announcing a manifestation of the Spirit. I clearly remember Carlo unpacking his cases as soon as he arrived. Splendid silk or nylon shirts appeared – I can still see them with their brilliant colours – and photographs from Fellini's film, *La strada*. I knew nothing of this film of Fellini's because I had been away from Italy for two years, and my inner being was in such turmoil that I had no time to take an interest in other things.

Carlo showed me the face of Gelsomina in the sort of stills one sees in cinema lobbies, to illustrate his decision.

I think the episode is important to an understanding of Carlo and the subsequent course of his life and his writing. He, a layman and teacher, could have fitted back into society like so many others did: he could have gone into politics or trade unionism or journalism. I know he had plenty of offers and many friends ready to help him and open up opportunities for him.

Other people who, like him, had held posts in Catholic Action and had gone through the same experience easily found employment, often in more important jobs, and they carried on working for the Kingdom outside the ranks of the Church.

I think that to understand Carlo completely, one must begin with his conversion. Today I understand that true conversion does not mean a switch from atheism to faith or from an immoral way of life to total obedience to the Law; above all it is the discovery that God's design is the only, definitive meaning of life. I have seen many pseudo-conversions which had absolutely no effect whatsoever on the meaning of life. I can safely say that the most important time in Carlo's life was the empty period between his resignation as Director and 4 November 1954. Fellini's film told his story: when he arrived he told me the plot of the film. Gelsomina's night-time conversation with the clown had made a deep impression on him: " 'Look,' says the young man, whose name I can't remember, to Gelsomina – 'this is a stone in the road. No one picks it up, no one stops to look at it, and yet the starlight falls on it, and so it is important.' "

Carlo had received the message: he had become a being without importance; he didn't become important right at that moment, but he could reflect a light coming from outside himself, from above.

My problem was similar to his: I too had been important, but I got the message later in a different way, which I have tried to describe in my book, *Facendo verità*.

We hadn't taken a joint decision to join the Fraternity; during our Roman encounters we merely talked about our frustration, and shared our feeling that we were both trapped in blind alleys.

The great temptation is to look for a way out; and if one looks carefully, it exists. But in that situation what takes real courage is to not run away, and to stop looking for temporary reasons for living. That way conversion doesn't seem to be the outcome of a voluntary decision – I hadn't practised my religion for many years, and from that day forwards I decided to start doing so again: I had not been obeying God's commandments, and from that day I renounced sin – but the decision came from on high. When we think of the miracle of Pentecost, we forget how it began: the bewilderment of the disciples, the discouragement that Luke detected in the two pilgrims on the road to Emmaus: "Jesus promised . . . so what shall we do now?"

Carlo spent his period in dry dock in a season without wind. That sort of deep faith – which he later proclaimed at the top of his voice to communities throughout Italy and the world, which waited eagerly for his visits and drew profound inspiration from his words – sprang, in Carlo's case, from what he went through before his novitiate; in my case it sprang from that dark night I spent in the novitiate.

He enthusiastically told me his great news over the phone. I have often thought of the similarity of our experiences, lived in such different contexts. The nausea which gripped Brother Charles of Jesus at the height of the parties he organized with such care, and which he prepared himself for as if they were events of great importance, was the same presage of conversion, the preamble to faith, which Carlo and I saw in that oh-so-blessed year of 1954.

Gelsomina discovered her musical rhythm, her inner harmony. Carlo would hum it to me while I was still sunk in my condition of the useless stone in the road, not yet lit by the rays of the star. In the desert we found the right person to help us in the period we were going through. When I think of Milad, our Master of Novices, I am reminded of the description of the Baptist – "What did you go out into the wilderness to look at?" (cf. Luke 7:24; Matthew 11:7). Milad did not wear a robe of camel's hair, nor did he eat locusts and wild honey. Actually he was more the friend of tax collectors, and enjoyed dining with "pagans" and "sinners", but the desert had stripped him completely of all those frills which conceal the Gospel, and yet are the boast of our Christian culture. The time I spent with Milad left me with a dislike for the words "training" and "trainer", because I realized that a master of novices has to resolve not to "train". I arrived from Rome intellectually and spiritually trained: I had mastered a vast amount of spiritual literature, and was very familiar with the role of trainer and guide for young people.

I wasn't dissatisfied with my work; unlike Carlo, I had ample opportunities open to me in the Church. I had no need to go hunting for a job with a political party or a trade union or some enterprise run by Catholic friends. I simply needed to break out of the carefully constructed armour I was living in, and which gave me a strong sense of security. We were two people coming to the desert from Rome: our lives had revolved around an association of about half a million enthusiastic young people who were willing to defend a cause without asking where exactly it fitted into the actual course of events.

When these young people finally did ask us for an explanation, we discovered ourselves to be prophets without a message.

Milad immediately sensed the difference between the two companions of venture. Carlo brought his identity with him in the photo of Gelsomina, with her frightened face, the emptiness in her eyes, her tousled hair and helplessness. This photo looked lost among the designer shirts and luxurious underwear that Carlo's Roman friends had bought for him – he who had never aspired to elegance. But the contents of those cases left Milad unmoved, because all that finery would easily disappear under the *abbaiah* and the *burnus* worn by all novices. A more serious problem was this priest with the spotless black cassock and the very high collar which forced him to look straight ahead with his nose in the air. He had left his luggage on an island in Brittany and arrived with only a bundle, but he was encased in a sort of steel breastplate. How to set him free? Contrary to what one would expect in a novitiate, the treatment was not the same for all. Carlo turned up already ingenuous, ready to receive the novelty of the message; he could write to his friends in Italy of the surprise he felt at living in the midst of nothing, with nothing.

He was able to describe the paradox of feeling that he was invited to look at the lilies and the grass of the field [cf. Matthew 6:28-30] and to have a heart full of joy, whereas I could only see emptiness and a void. Milad asked me not to write and not to read; to become almost illiterate. It wasn't a law or a rule, it was the star's ray which was trying to reach me. Gelsomina's friend had told Carlo the story of the stone, and Carlo had been convinced by it; the story described his own experience. For me the ray of the star could only act like a laser and smash the metal bonds of my prison. If I had recorded all the words spoken to me by Milad in thirteen months of living together, I wouldn't be able to fill a single type-written page. But just to see him and listen to his readings from the Gospel made me realize how complicated and bombastic that man "clothed in all his glory" was, only to be reduced to silence and hopelessly humbled before the image of John the Baptist. Since he arrived later, Carlo did not join the same group of novices as I; we lived in the same place, we took part in the same events, but I belonged to a group which was preparing to take its vows at an earlier date than Carlo's.

The community of novices was divided into small groups called chapters. Within these chapters we had the opportunity to communicate on a deeper level and hence gain a greater knowledge of each other's individual traits, and Carlo was not in any of my chapters. But I knew Carlo profoundly, and our brief meetings and his nearness during the long afternoons spent in silent adoration were of great comfort to me.

Several times, during these fleeting encounters, I asked him: "Carlo, what do you say to the Lord?" His eyes would fill with that childlike joy which said far more than his words. I told him about my experience of God as an enemy, because it was many months before I surrendered.

Knowing Carlo, I know that the experience of sweetness and joy he told me of was not the whole truth. At the time when he was in charge of the Gioventù he had acquired the knack of transmitting enthusiasm and the joy of serving a cause in which he believed absolutely to young people, and he had learned to keep his troubles, of which he certainly had plenty, to himself. I know that the desert wasn't easy, even for him; he told me this one night when we were praying together. The howls of the jackals, which sounded like women in fits of hysteria, made us shudder physically. But the Psalms lent him words of faith and comfort, which he repeated for many years to all the discouraged hearts which crossed his path. The Friend bestowed on him, who was so much simpler than I, that vision which was conceded to me later on – "Blessed are the eyes that see what you see" (Luke 10:23) – and he felt free to share this experience, which filled the long hours of the novitiate, with so many friends. *Lettere dal deserto* will always be his essential message.

One of his favourite tasks in the novitiate was to cook: the kitchen at El-Abiodh was not wonderful, but Carlo knew how to get the best use out of the little available, so that he always produced something new with an unusual flavour. At the Saturday assemblies Milad, as Master of Novices, would hand out our weekly tasks, and when he announced: "and in the kitchen . . . Carlo", the community instantly felt cheered. Milad, who had the strong sense of humour common in spiritual people, would slyly draw out the words: ". . . and in the kitchen . . ." – and finally the name of the great chef – ". . . Carlo."

I used to catch glimpses of him at the big stove, hot and happy; I would see the Carlo of the old days, surrounded by youngsters, distributing smiles and companionship: "Today I'm going to prepare you a moment of happiness."

One day Milad entrusted him with a delicate and important mission. Some Arab dignitaries were invited to the Fraternity and Milad wanted to offer them tea and cakes, knowing the guests' passion for sweet things, and so Carlo had to prove himself an able pastry-cook. About four that afternoon three magnificent cakes were displayed on the refectory tables. Carlo was at adoration, recuperating his silence after spending all that energy and care on his unusual task. The novices knew nothing about the secret pact between Milad and Carlo, and they thought this was a loving surprise for them, so the cakes almost completely disappeared into their ravenous stomachs.

That evening, when Milad summoned the pastry-cook to serve tea and slices of cake to his guests, poor Carlo found only the sorry remains. News of the disaster spread rapidly and everybody expected that there would be all hell to pay at the evening assembly. I believe Milad never once showed signs of losing his temper, but he knew how to be severe and unbending in cases where he detected people wandering from the way of Christ. That night he commented on what had happened by putting on such an enjoyable show that I don't think any of us have ever forgotten it since. He depicted Carlo, taking great pains over the preparation of those cakes, his masterpieces, only for wolves to get into the kitchen and scoff the lot – and the poor, crestfallen pastry-cook has to present himself empty-handed. If I close my eyes, I can still hear Milad's voice, which is just about to burst into laughter and sweep his whole audience with him. This episode has been very useful to me in my life, warning me when I am tempted to attach too much importance to things which aren't important at all. Naturally, there followed a long interval without the chef. For a few weeks the words, "and in the kitchen . . ." waited in vain for the name we all wanted to hear – "Carlo" – because, despite their obvious good faith, the novices had indulged in extremely untimely greed.

Then we were separated: I took part in the *khaloua*, the 500-kilometre pilgrimage from El-Abiodh to Béni Abbès, which was the central event of the novitiate and was a great turning-point for me: God the enemy became God the friend. Carlo made this pilgrimage a few months later and he stayed on in the desert, recording his experiences for the numerous readers who were attracted by his limpid and direct style of writing.

I met him again several times in the years that followed: we were both passionately involved in profoundly different experiences. Carlo was deeply frustrated by our prosperous society, and I by the problem of the Third World. We had in common our way of seeing the Church from outside, from the standpoint of the people we worked among. We both wanted – and why not speak for him too? – a Church which would keep its promise to satisfy the truly serious needs of mankind today. Not a Church which worries about cakes so that important people invited to tea won't feel a little dissatisfied, but one that is concerned about real hunger. We talked about our mutual indignation, stemming from different experiences and from the same consuming love for the Kingdom. The same love that enveloped him in a wave of harmony when he passed to eternal life on 4 October 1988, the same day on which St Francis died. Our great Brother [Carlo] made it known that he was not displeased by the comparison, in his book, *Io, Francesco*.

The comparison between the great Francis and little Carlo is not an unsuitable one, since St Paul the Apostle remarked that one star shines brighter than another, but still they are both stars (cf. 1 Corinthians 15:41).

APPENDIX 4

Brother Milad Aïssa (1912–84)

The letters we have chosen show how deeply Milad's sudden death affected our Fraternity (of Little Brothers and Little Sisters). This event roused "feelings which are extremely difficult to describe", but the suffering it caused certainly brought more grace with it than sadness. This testifies to what Milad was and still is: not the "servant" but the "friend" of Jesus, as it says in the Gospel (John 15); a passage which he himself commented on several times. It is also his role in the life and history of the Fraternity.

He arrived in El-Abiodh in 1935, two years after it was founded. His gift to the "Ouled Sidi Cheikh" was a reflection of his gift to God: without taint or second thoughts. The physical and spiritual roots he put down gave the life of the Fraternity the benefit of his wealth of human experience and supernatural wisdom, as well as a deeply personal note. During the most crucial years of the Fraternity's growth, Milad was Brother René Voillaume's deputy and Master of Novices. But his light was to shine far beyond this period in time and far beyond our religious family.

El-Abiodh, 11 December 1984

From Michel Sainte Beuve
Prior of the Little Brothers of Jesus

Brothers,

Milad has left us suddenly, and yesterday we buried him in the cemetery in the garden, next to Maurice T., who died in 1956. He is the fifth Brother to be buried here, witness to the fifty-one years that the Fraternity has been in El-Abiodh.

Milad's death was very swift. His heart stopped beating after another attack: the first happened a few years ago.

For him, his death was truly magnificent. He was just about to celebrate the Eucharist and he found himself face to face with his Lord on the morning of the Feast of the Immaculate Conception. But you can imagine what a terrible shock it was for the Brothers and Sisters, and all the friends of El-Abiodh! When it happened, Jean-Michel, Raymond, Haroon, as well as Teo and Taher, who were doing their "year in the desert", were at the Fraternity. The Little Sisters of the El-Abiodh Fraternity were also there, and those living in the Fraternities among the nomads arrived soon after. I was in Tamanrasset after General Chapter. I was just back from London, at the end of a two-month stay in Assekrem.

The funeral was held on 10 December. The whole Christian community of the neighbourhood was there: the Sisters and Brothers of Béni Abbès, Oran, Algiers and Le Bissa; the White Fathers, our French associates, Egyptians, Indians . . . It isn't a very large community, but once again I felt the unity and vitality of this little Church of Algeria. The Bishop of Oran, Pierre Claverie, came instead of the Bishop of the Sahara, who was in Egypt. Many friends from among the inhabitants of El-Abiodh came to pay their respects, which they did more during personal meetings and visits, where they could speak freely, than at the actual funeral.

Milad came to El-Abiodh in 1935; and he lived here for forty-nine years without ever being away for any length of time. Reflecting on the long time he spent here, I realized that he stood for the history and the growth of the Fraternity, just as he did for the human community in which he lived. And after fifty years, this history and this development have been shaken to the core!

To borrow a phrase from the recent Chapter, I said to myself that Milad was with us for a long time as "one who stays alert" (cf. Luke 12:37), both on a personal level, and as regards the Fraternity as a whole. He was able to make us feel, discover and rediscover the ways of the Lord with his words and even more, with the example of his life. He had a dynamism which helped others to open themselves to the Spirit and overcome their fears and apprehensions. For all of us his death provides an opportunity to thank the Lord for having given us Milad for these past fifty years, and to thank him for all the light that we have received thanks to his presence. As soon as possible we shall be compiling Milad's writings and talks for circulation. This is the best way, it seems to me, to help us preserve his memory and the meaning of his presence alive amongst us for ever.

An extract from the draft of the Constitutions written by Milad in 1981:

But whatever form our death may take, we must know that our vocation as disciples of Jesus is to share his suffering, and so we shall also share in his glory (cf. Romans 8:17), so that we may praise the Lord our God, in the communion of saints, all together, for all eternity.

"Blessed are those who are invited to the marriage supper of the Lamb" (Revelation 19:9).

"Come, Lord Jesus!" (22:20).

At sea, 16 December 1984

From René Voillaume
Founder of the Little Brothers of Jesus

Brothers,

In Marrakech, on 10 December, the Brothers gave me the news of Brother Milad's sudden and unexpected death. I had left him eight days before in perfect health. It took me several days to realize that his absence is final and that I shall never see him again on this earth.

Providence decreed that during those last few days we spent together we were very close. I called on him to give him those pages on El-Abiodh's history that he didn't yet have, especially those in which I gave a detailed account of the important role he played in the founding of the Fraternity. We were bound by very close ties in those days, particularly between 1946 and 1950, when we shared responsibility for the Fraternity. We owe the training of the early generations of Brothers to him. I reread the long, detailed and friendly letters he wrote me at the time, with great joy. When writing up that period in the history of El-Abiodh I had hesitated over including some long passages from his letters because of their personal nature, but now I don't regret it at all.

During those last days, just before leaving, I had asked him for the umpteenth time to write his memoirs and to round off – and correct if necessary – what I had written about that period in the Fraternity's history, and in the end he promised he would get to work on it.

His relationship with the people of El-Abiodh was wonderful. Having arrived in El-Abiodh in 1935, next year Milad would have celebrated half a century spent in this patch of desert.

As I write these lines aboard the boat taking me back to Sete, I still don't know the exact circumstances of his death or how the local people reacted to it, but I can easily imagine. However, I wanted to write to you about Milad's death without delay, since I have to set off again for Bangui in a couple of days' time.

As regards my personal feelings, I'm sure you completely understand what the passing of a fellow-traveller of those early years, and of one who was one of the last remaining witnesses of the life of the El-Abiodh Fraternity through all its phases, means to me. It is hard for me to describe my feelings properly, maybe because they are too deep for that.

And finally, the circumstances of Milad's death remind us once more that the Lord comes to take us back when we least expect it. Several times, in Zaïre, in Mexico and in the Ahaggar Mountains, the Lord has come looking for our Brothers.

El-Abiodh-Sidi-Cheikh, 14 December 1984

From some Little Brothers
and Little Sisters of El-Abiodh

Dear Brothers, Sisters and friends,

This letter is addressed to all of you who knew our brother Milad Aïssa. Six days have already elapsed since Jesus came looking for him "like a thief"; six days during which we have had very little time for writing; but we want to share our Brother's final moments with you without putting it off any longer. We are aware, as our friends in the village often remind us, that Milad didn't only belong to us; he is yours too.

Yes, Jesus came "like a thief". On 7 December, Milad was still making heaps of long- and short-term plans. He had offered to drive a Brother, who was to spend eight days in a hermitage ninety kilometres from El-Abiodh, over the desert on the morning of the 8th. They were expecting him in Béni Abbès on the 11th to hold a retreat for the Little Sisters, and from there he wanted to go to Timimoun with one of his friends from El-Abiodh.

Yes, Jesus came looking for him "like a thief", but we are convinced that Milad was ready for this meeting and that he said to his "Beloved Brother and Lord Jesus": "Here I am!"

At seven o'clock on the morning of 8 December, the Immaculate Conception of Mary, Milad was in the chapel, about to celebrate the Eucharist with three Brothers (Raymond, Haroon and Teo) and two Little Sisters (Alice and Geneviève-Emmanuelle). The evening before, he had asked Teo to lead the Gloria, the Alleluia and, at the end of Mass, the Magnificat, despite the small number of singers. He wanted to celebrate the Virgin Mary's feast joyfully.

As usual here, the Office is read before Holy Communion. Thus, after the hymn and Psalm 62, the Brothers and Sisters began "The Song of the Three Holy Children": "Bless the Lord, all you works of the Lord; sing praise to him and highly exalt him forever . . . Bless the Lord, you angels of the Lord . . ." (Azariah 1:35-37). At that moment Milad felt a pain in his chest and he asked Little Sister Geneviève-Emmanuelle, who is a doctor, to accompany him to his room.[1]

From that moment, things moved rapidly. In the time it took to get some medicine and call another doctor (an Algerian), Milad was already with Mary, the mother of Jesus and his mother too, together with the chosen and all the heavenly throng, celebrating the "marriage of the Lamb" mentioned by St John in Revelation (19:5 et seq.).

Yes, Jesus came "like a thief", but Milad was ready for his visit. We found it very difficult to take in what had happened because things went so fast. The following day, during the liturgy of the second

Sunday of Advent, the Apostle Peter reminded us: "The day of the Lord will come like a thief" [2 Peter 3:10].

Jean-Michel had left the evening before to take Taher to the Mulk Sliman hermitage. A friend from El-Abiodh went to meet him on his way home, to tell him the news of Milad's death. He immediately turned back to fetch Taher, whom he had left in his solitude. When they reached the Fraternity in the early afternoon, a lot of friends from the village had already come to see Milad for the last time: men, women and children. We heard them calling Milad "our father", "our brother", "our friend"; they told us: "Milad isn't only yours, he is ours too." He had loved them, listened to them, given them advice, cared for them and helped them in so many ways . . . Many wept for him, as one would for a father. We were getting ready to celebrate his fifty years at El-Abiodh next year, on 13 October. Together the Brothers and Sisters welcomed all those people.

To begin with, Milad's body was laid out in his room, his face as calm as if he were asleep; later, he was placed in the chapel and there we celebrated Holy Communion at eight in the evening. His friends filed past him until he was buried on the afternoon of the 10th, at four o'clock.

A group of fifty-four Christians of the Church of Algeria accompanied Milad to the cemetery of the Brothers and Sisters in our garden, where he was buried next to Brother Maurice.

We also received a great many telegrams and letters. These showed us to what extent Milad was not "only ours". At Holy Communion on 8 December, in the Basilica of Notre Dame d'Afrique, Cardinal Duval spoke of this Brother of ours who had had such an impact on the Church of Algeria. Yes, we are convinced that this grain of wheat fallen into the earth will bear much fruit (cf. John 12:24).

At the cemetery, a Coptic-Catholic Egyptian friend sang the Gospel text about the Day of Judgement in St Matthew (25:31-46) in Arabic; and at Holy Communion we sang the beatitudes from St Matthew's Gospel (5:1-12).

On the occasion of his death, we were able to see for ourselves just how greatly this life, given entirely to God and his Brothers, was evangelical and rich in contradiction, through and through. True love, "that which bears the mark of God", Milad wrote, cannot leave one indifferent, "because in the end, in the depths of the heart, it insists on a response".

We have not yet fully realized how great was the grace God bestowed on us by allowing us to live in such close proximity to this "man of God", who was a father, brother, friend and sure guide to us.

APPENDIX 5

Testimonials

From Yoel Nathan, a Little Brother of Jesus in Israel:
I arrived in El-Abiodh right after Christmas 1954; at the time there were a lot of candidates for the novitiate (perhaps twenty-five or thirty) arriving in successive waves; there was no set date for beginning the novitiate.

Carlo stood out among the novices who were there before me, by virtue of his age; I don't think any of us were over thirty, whereas Carlo was already well over forty, and his white hair gave him away. Despite the local clothing (*jellhabad, burnous* and *cheche*) which we all wore, without doubt he was the one who could never easily pass for an Arab! Despite his age and the important position he had held in Italy, Carlo received no "special treatment" and Milad, our Master of Novices, paid no particular attention to him.

Life in the novitiate was very simple, rough and austere. Carlo's behaviour matched this simplicity, and was seasoned with friendliness and a lot of good humour, and we all felt comfortable with him, as if we were equals. For Carlo, joining the Fraternity meant a radical change in his life. He confronted the stages of this spiritual process of divestment, long and silent prayer, closeness to Jesus and evangelical life, with enthusiasm. He gave the impression of having found the priceless pearl of the Gospel, the solid rock, compared to which everything that he had known before seemed trivial. While for most of the Brothers, Father de Foucauld's message – as we tried to live it in the Fraternity – seemed essentially a personal vocation, Carlo saw it on a far wider scale, as an invitation to renew the life of the Church.

Here are some other memories I have of him. One of the tasks assigned to the novices was to bake bread; I was initiated to it by Carlo. We had to light the fire (bundles of sticks, dry branches and so on), mix the dough and knead it. When it had risen and the oven was hot enough, the loaves were put into it on long paddles. I still remember how Carlo did all this, competent and completely absorbed.

Later he was assigned to shoe-making and he made good sandals, cutting the soles out of old tyres. During his novitiate Carlo received a visit from his brother, a Salesian bishop who was a missionary in Thailand. I felt that a bishop visiting El-Abiodh was something of an event, but the way Carlo behaved with him did away with all my preconceived ideas of protocol and the reverential awe I felt was a bishop's due. Of course, he was Carlo's younger brother. Right from the day after his arrival Carlo had made him swap his cassock for one of our *jellhabads*, and today I can still see the pair of them, sitting side by side on the cart hauled by our old mare, on the way to the Géryville caves where we spent days of solitude and prayer: this little bishop needed "training"! (I have to admit that the little bishop let Carlo take over with extreme docility.)

One last memory – rather a painful one – is of the wretched intramuscular injection which ought to have been given intravenously . . . or maybe the real problem was that the medicine was off. Anyway, the muscles in Carlo's leg wasted and he suffered from it for the rest of his life. It was a tremendous blow, but I recall that Carlo never harboured any resentment towards the nursing Brother, and treated him and everybody else with his usual good humour.

From Claude Collet, a Little Brother of Jesus in France:
Carlo arrived at the El-Abiodh novitiate almost at the same time as Arturo Paoli, and they brought us their experience of the Church, which interested us all, since Carlo and Arturo had lived very close to the Pope, the cardinals and so forth . . . That was a period of missionary, as well as theological and spiritual, ferment. It was clear that by deciding to enter the Fraternity, they both wanted to break with Italian Catholic Action, to which they had given a great deal of themselves. However, the spirituality of the Fraternity, insofar as it implies a certain relationship between the Church and the rest of

the world, seemed to satisfy them as the final goal of their long search.

Today I am unable to recall this or that interesting conversation we had then, but I have a very clear memory of Carlo. His cheerfulness in the context of life in the novitiate – which inevitably produces tensions – triggered off some extremely salutary moments of fun!

What more can I say after so many years? Oh yes: the memory of a man of God – a true one!

From Jacques Wilhelm, a Little Brother of the Gospel in Tanzania:
I am pleased to hear that you are about to bring out an edition of some of Carlo's unpublished writings; I shall try to come up with some memories of the time I spent with him in the novitiate at El-Abiodh; of course, they may be rather confused after thirty-three years! . . . Has it really been that long?

Carlo began his novitiate with a large group – about twenty-five novices – and I believe at least twenty of them saw it through to the end. I myself started my novitiate in April 1955, so I didn't even spend a whole year with Carlo. Charlie Rotsart, who was also called to become a Little Brother of the Gospel later on (those two congregations!), lived in Tamanrasset with Carlo for many years, the desert years . . . He would be a superb witness, but I know he doesn't write at all or, at least, very little . . .

Arturo Paoli was a novice at El-Abiodh too at the time, and so he and Carlo could claim to be the first two Italian Little Brothers. There were also a few Spaniards, Belgians, Brasilians, Vietnamese, French and me from Switzerland . . . There were a lot of people at El-Abiodh in that period, perhaps the most the Fraternity ever had at one time.

Milad was assisted by Emmanuel Brun (Manu di Grenay), who acted as Vice-Master of Novices.

The fact that Carlo and Arturo had been in the top echelons of Italian Catholic Action was well known to us all, but neither of them let it show in any way, and they behaved with the same simplicity and openness as all the other novices.

I recall Carlo making very rudimentary sandals with soles cut from car tyres (here in Tanzania they are still all the rage!). I can see him with his big smile and affability, greeting a new novice on his arrival, and immediately measuring his feet so as to make him a well-fitting a pair of sandals as he could . . . and he was very good at it. He also used to make bread in our oven . . . He was always on time for all the spiritual exercises which punctuated our day. When it was permitted, he loved to chat with the other Brothers, and these were always occasions of great warmth.

We shared with him the difficult moment of the accident to his leg, caused by the nursing Brother on duty giving him the wrong injection – or perhaps the medicine which was injected had gone off – the instructions were written in German . . . The fact remains that Carlo's leg was damaged for the rest of his life. It was my turn to do the nursing right after the incident and so, having taken care of Carlo personally, I can state that I never heard him complain once . . . That is all for now!

Mario Fumagalli

Father Mario Fumagalli was born in Bernareggio in 1931 and before entering a seminary at the age of twenty-three, he had worked as a plasterer. "When I discovered that God existed," he said in an interview, "there was nothing I could do but follow him, step by step, in what he himself had done in Nazareth." Therefore he joined the Congregation of the Little Brothers of Charles de Foucauld and spent his novitiate in El-Abiodh in the Algerian Sahara.

As a Little Brother he worked in several countries: with the people of the oases, then as a miner in Belgium, then as a nurse in France (while he was studying), and then as a farm labourer in the rice paddies of Japan.

When he arrived in Livorno to found a Fraternity of his congregation there, he worked as a labourer on a building site, but through contact with the priests of the Opera della Madonnina del Grappa, he decided to see his religious vocation right through and become a diocesan priest. He finished his theological studies, begun in Toulouse, and was ordained to the priesthood by Cardinal Florit in Florence on 29 June 1969.

An interview published in IL FOCOLARE
Don't you think . . . perhaps you made a mistake in becoming a diocesan priest, when you already had such special religious and social experience. Why did you do it?

I shall tell you why I did it. I am a manual worker and until I was twenty-three I was a plasterer. When I discovered that God existed, there was nothing I could do – literally – but follow him, step by step, in what he himself had done in Nazareth.

The problem was finding the way to develop my vocation, which was to be truly like Jesus in Nazareth. I made enquiries, and heard of the existence of the religious family of de Foucauld in France, so I applied to join them.

For me, at that time, it was my only chance of an adult vocation because I lacked any kind of cultural or religious education. Moreover, I hated the clergy and seminaries: I wouldn't have found it easy to accept the kind of life which seminarists led twenty years ago. Then I went exactly where I didn't want to go, but since God put me there, I am content.

Your early years with the Little Brothers certainly gave you an opportunity for spiritual growth and experience with people: how do you intend to fulfil the aims which were formative in your youth?

My Fraternity experience helped me considerably to intensify a life of consecration to God and to serve people, irrespective of class, race or nationality, and particularly the poor and the outcasts from society. To serve God and serve mankind by giving oneself, or rather, one's life: this is Christian, and it can be done anywhere. I learned that the Good News is not only meant for specialists who retreat from the world; on the contrary, it is by going out into the world that the Gospel is fulfilled, and by being ready for anything that God and mankind may ask of me today. Becoming a priest means, for me, the achievement of those very goals I had set myself, only with greater intensity and fulfilment.

As a Little Brother you made a considerable number of contacts in Europe, Africa and the Far East. Will you tell us your impression of them and how they enriched your spirit?

As a Little Brother I had the chance to live in many different parts of the world. In the Algerian desert, working with the people of the oases. In the hell of the Belgian coal mines (at the time of the Marcinelle disaster!) as a miner for a couple of years. While I was studying in France, I took any work that was offered me: farm hand, nurse, etc. In Japan I worked as a labourer in the rice paddies.

Learning physical and human geography through direct and personal contact, and not just from books, has shown me just how unchristian our sense of justice is. The Third World exists in the Belgian mines as well, where thousands of workers are exploited, because advantage is taken of the fact that they are immigrants from countries which are unable to offer them work at home.

In Japan I lived with a number of peasant families. In general the peoples of the East, and Japan in particular, are disconcerting. Compared to them we are crude. The Japanese work hard and love culture; they are greatly attached to their families and adore their children. Respectful, polite, ready to help others without being asked, they take every opportunity to fete guests or neighbours. They are very loyal to each other. For example, farming villages own machinery, mills and so on in common. They swop days of work, depending on the demands of the season.

During my little journey round the world I have never come across a people as friendly, sensitive or refined as the Japanese.

You did your novitiate with the Little Brothers at El-Abiodh in the Algerian Sahara, with Carlo Carretto and Arturo Paoli. What can you tell us of the time you spent with the two friends?

I didn't know Carlo Carretto and Arturo Paoli at all before. My meeting with them in the novitiate at El-Abiodh was a new experience, from every point of view. For them, the discovery of the social and religious value of work was the main topic of every conversation. For me, work had always been my only means of survival, and was nothing new. What I was looking for in the desert was my life with God, or in other words, what God's will was in me: work wasn't a problem as far as I was concerned; it was my daily bread. In our unity we were divided, and we were attracted to two different poles. The problem of the workers was a part of my life; I was in search of God and the Church. I should like to say that – in my case – it was not the Church going to the world of work, but the worker going in search of the Church. However, the year in the desert was a voyage of discovery for us all. They were Italians with an Italian Catholic mentality. I had given up everything; I wanted to meet and find out about other people who saw things from a different point of view, and who lived a Christian life in harmony with their physical surroundings. De Foucauld's discovery is a valid one in my opinion: it is the man of God who gives himself entirely to mankind. To become an Arab among the Arabs was not easy: we whites were colonialists and they, the Arabs, were deprived of their freedom; therefore our presence was questionable. The novitiate was the European way of life, transplanted in Africa; that particular brand of European life-style, in fact, which is French. My relationship with Carlo and Arturo remained one between foreigners; any attempt to form groups of the same nationality was, according to our superiors, a threat to the universality of the Fraternity, even though this universality was effectively limited to being French.

Notes

NOTE TO THE INTRODUCTION

1. Except in a few places where the sand is heaped in dunes, most of the desert consists of a rocky terrain scattered with stones. These stony areas are called *reg*. When a large area is covered with sand dunes, some of which may be extremely high, it is called *erg*.

NOTE TO THE PREFACE

Gian Carlo Sibilia was born in Tripoli, Libya, in 1934. His education and subsequent career have both been in the entrepreneurial field. In the sixties he held an executive post in the GIAC and he has been active in Church organizations in Italy and abroad. He is a member of the Charles de Foucauld Family, and in 1970 he became presbyter of the Church of Foligno, where he holds a number of posts.

He is the Prior of the Little Brothers and Little Sisters of the Comunità Jesus Caritas and he is also the editor of the spiritual magazine, *Famiglia Charles de Foucauld*. For over twenty-five years he was a close friend of Carlo Carretto, who entrusted him with the editing of his letters, spiritual diaries and notes.

DECEMBER NOTES

1. "Seeing me leave for Africa, some people thought I was suffering from an attack of depression and renunciation. Nothing could be further from the truth.

"The political exploitation of Catholic Action was a major factor in my decision, but it was not the principal motive. I was so enthusiastic about Catholic Action and my whole involvement in it that I wouldn't have left for anything.

"And God made me empty inside. He said: 'You are no longer doing any good.'

"I realized that I wasn't capable of converting anyone any more – I was no longer effective.

"The Lord managed to pull me out of there because I had lost faith in myself, in the organization and in the movement. I felt drained and told myself: 'I am dead here.' But when faith began to move within me, I realized that perhaps in him was a new fruitfulness. I had no experience, I simply planned to 'live in faith'. 'Live in faith and you'll see that something will happen.' While politics was telling us, 'You are powerful,' the voice of Jesus was growing stronger within me: 'Without me you can do nothing.' " (Teresio Bosco, *Carlo Carretto*, Elle Di Ci, Turin, 1980, pp. 9-15.)

Perhaps it has not yet been made sufficiently clear that Carretto's crisis, and Mario Rossi's later on, cannot be confined to a single political interpretation, particularly apparent during the Sturzo affair. It must also be viewed with the Church in mind. In 1949 Carlo wrote in his diary: "30 September – Catholic Action is suffering from senility and is in danger of seizing up due to its excessive rules and regulations. If it carries on like this the apostolate will switch to other, younger organizations, less endowed with statutes, but more able to capture the message of the Spirit with the simplicity of intuition. However, it is a shame this is happening because I have truly loved Catholic Action, as one might care for a sweetheart." And again: "11 October – Motherhood of Mary – Subiaco – A place which is dear to me for its spiritual riches. Three days with the other staff members. Increasingly I feel the need to relinquish my position as Director of the GIAC [Gioventù Italiana di Azione Cattolica]. Soon it will be necessary to train my successor. Be it a defect in the organization, be it my fault, but I am no longer the right man to represent this association. I have immersed myself with great joy in Fr Paoli's reflections on humility. I long for solitude! But often this wish is tainted by laziness and cowardice. I feel I am still a beginner." (*Fondo Carretto/Jesus Caritas*. See Appendix 1.)

2. *Liliana Carretto* (b. 1925), married to a lawyer, Mario Turchi (1925-90). She was the youngest member of the Carretto family, which consisted of father Luigi (1879-1971), mother Maria Rovea (1887-1960), two sisters who joined the Daughters of Our Lady Help of Christians – Sister Paola Emerenziana (b. 1907) and Sister Dolcidia (1908-86) – Brother Carlo (1910-88), the Salesian Bishop Mgr Pietro (b. 1912) and Vittorio (1917-19).

3. *Poldo and Nino:* Leopoldo Saletti (b. 1913) and Giovanni Testa (b. 1915) were among Carlo's dearest friends from the years they spent together in the Salesian Oratory at the Crocetta di Torino in their youth. They followed Carlo to Rome when he accepted the Directorate of the Gioventù Italiana branch of Catholic Action. Together with Carlo they

helped found (in 1954) the "Nive Candidior" Mountain Refuge in Cervinia.

"My dream was to go to the Alps and practise Fraternity among the Alpine guides who help those in trouble during bad weather on Mount Cervino.

"Dreams are not born by chance. I had always been a climber. I was a captain in the Alpine troops and the mountains were my passion. I wanted to dedicate my passion to helping my brothers in difficulties in the snow. I enjoyed establishing Fraternity with the guides and devoting my prayers and my services to that far-from-easy task, as prompted by Jesus. But it was a dream." (From *Perché Sognare?*, Morcelliana, Brescia, 1985, pp. 10-11.)

4. *Henry Marthieu* (1914-88): a French presbyter (1939). He was a Little Brother (1953) at the Marseilles Fraternity-Secretariat in the Rue Tapis-Vert, in an area notorious for prostitution and crime.

5. *Saint-Maximin:* a small town to the north-east of Marseilles. There was a Fraternity for Little Brothers of Jesus living in groups of five or six in tiny apartments, and attending lectures in philosophy and theology at the School of the Dominican Fathers. The rural surroundings provided employment for the student Brothers in the great vineyards of the region. For some years Saint-Maximin was also a Fraternity for novices; now it houses Little Brothers in need of rest.

6. *Berre* (France). Brother René Voillaume writes: "The first working Fraternity of the Little Brothers of Jesus was founded at Aix-en-Provence in 1947, but the following year it moved to Berre-l'Etang, an industrial city on the banks of the Etang de Berre about twenty kilometres from Aix. Large numbers of workers, mainly from North Africa, were employed at the oil refinery or other chemical firms, and they thronged the old parts of the city. In one of these crumbling houses the Little Brothers set up their Fraternity. The new practice within the Church whereby religious or priests work for wages on construction sites or for outside concerns was allowed by only a few bishops in those days. Charles de Provenchères, Archbishop of Aix, not only gave his permission, but introduced this novelty into the religious life of the Fraternity with enthusiasm." Carlo went back to this Fraternity immediately after his novitiate (1956-57). Today the Berre Fraternity is closed.

7. *La Cappellette:* an area of Marseilles where there was a Postulant Fraternity of the Little Brothers of Jesus (1952-63).

8. *Oran* (Onahran in Arabic): a university and diocesan city with over

a million inhabitants, and Algeria's second largest port. Here Carlo had his first encounter with the religious life of the Little Brothers of Jesus – there was a Fraternity in the port area. Today the Fraternity is closed.

9 *Santa Cruz* (Bordij El Djebel in Arabic): a fort built by the Spanish in the sixteenth century, about 400 metres above sea level. There is a stupendous view of the city of Oran and of its beaches and port.

10. *Saïda:* an Algerian city with approximately 100,000 inhabitants lying at an altitude of 850 metres in the heart of a fertile and well-irrigated region.

11. *Géryville* (El Bayadh in Arabic): an Algerian city of around 60,000 inhabitants, 1,320 metres above sea level. It was settled in 1852 and is famous for its carpet industry and for the presence in the area of about a million sheep, goats, camels and oxen. It lies 100 kilometres from El-Abiodh and was a compulsory stop on the way to the novitiate.

12. *The White Fathers:* The Society of Missionaries of Africa. It was founded in 1868 by Cardinal Charles Lavigerie (1825-92), Archbishop of Algiers. Charles de Foucauld and his spiritual family owe them a great debt of gratitude.

13. *El-Abiodh-Sidi-Cheikh* (usually known simply as *El-Abiodh*) lies on the plateau (903 metres above sea level) in the south of Oran province. It is an Islamic holy place where people come on pilgrimage to the tomb of Sidi Cheikh, the famous seventeenth-century Marabout. The population is poor, in part nomadic and in part settled.

In 1933 an old military fort became the "mother house" of a new religious order following in the footsteps of Charles de Foucauld: the Little Brothers and the Little Sisters of Jesus. (See Appendix 2.)

The Little Brothers and Little Sisters of Jesus are still to be found in El-Abiodh today. (Cf. Carlo Carretto, *Lettere a Dolcidia*, Citadella, Assisi, 1989, pp. 23-52.)

14. *Arturo Paoli* (b. 1912): a teacher of philosophy from Tuscany. During the last war he was also a Partisan and an active member of the Liberation Committee working for the Jews. He served as the Presbyter of the Church of Lucca (1940) and was called to Rome to serve as Chief Deputy of the GIAC during Carlo Carretto's and Mario Rossi's terms of office. After serving as chaplain aboard a ship carrying Italian emigrants to Argentina, he entered the novitiate at El-Abiodh a few months earlier than Carlo. Today he is a Little Brother of the Gospel in southern Brazil, sharing the life of farming cooperatives with groups of volunteers and local families. (See Appendix 3. Cf. Arturo Paoli, *Facendo Verità*, Gribaudi, Turin, 1984.)

15. *René Voillaume* (b. 1905): a French presbyter (1929). In 1933 he and four other young presbyters founded a new congregation based on the rule of Charles de Foucauld. (Cf. René Voillaume, *Come loro*, Paoline, Rome, 1953.)

16. *Milad:* Onésime Retailleau (1912-84), a French Little Brother. He made his religious vows on 25 December 1936, taking the name of Brother Natale. He became a presbyter in 1939. At the beginning of the fifties, on the insistence of his settled and nomadic friends, his name was changed to Milad Aïssa, which literally means "the birth of Christ" in Arabic. (See Appendix 4.)

17. (See Appendix 5.)

18. *Gelsomina* is a character played by Giulietta Masina in Federico Felini's film, *La strada*. (See Appendix 3.)

19. *Moncalieri* (Turin), where the Carretto family moved from Alessandria, Piedmont (1912-23). Later they moved from Moncalieri to Turin. In Moncalieri Carlo was confirmed and received First Communion. While still a boy he began working to pay for his education, first as an errand boy for a carpenter and then as a sexton and a night watchman for a family.

". . . and that was how they went to Alessandria, where I was born, followed two years later by my brother. They left Alessandria for Moncalieri, which had a far more suitable environment for us to spend our poverty-stricken adolescence in. It was a suburb of the city which had a bit of everything, but above all everything we needed . . . I was born in Alessandria like that . . . by chance. Alessandria was my parents' temporary home when they were first married, having left their own part of the country. They also left behind the peasant culture that, thank God, the family had enjoyed for generation after generation . . ." (From *Ho cercato e ho trovato*, Cittadella, Assisi, 1983, pp. 21-25.)

20. Q. Brother, what do you ask?

A. I ask to be admitted among the Little Brothers of Jesus.

Q. Are you ready, for the sake of the Gospel of Jesus, not only to live in poverty, owning nothing, but also to accept the condition of the poor who are obliged to work in order to live, in fulfilment of divine law?

A. I sincerely wish to be poor for Jesus and for the Gospel.

Q. Are you ready to learn to willingly obey God and those in authority over you in his name, because Jesus was obedient till death, and because you wish to work with him to redeem your brothers?

A. I truly desire to submit to all obedience, for Jesus' sake and for the salvation of my brothers.

Q. Are you willing to pray every day with faith and courage, in harmony with the Eucharist, and to continue despite difficulties, to trust in the promises Jesus made about prayer?

A. I promise it to Jesus through his sacrament, and I shall ask him to help me.

Q. Are you ready, following the example of Brother Charles of Jesus, your guide and your help, to sacrifice everything and go wherever obedience sends you?

A. I wish to love all people without discouragement, trusting for strength in the love of Jesus, master of the impossible.

21. Carlo visited Bethlehem for the first time in 1952, after two long world tours which took him to Spain, Morocco, Algeria, Brazil, Argentina, Uruguay, Greece, Syria, Lebanon, Saudi Arabia, Pakistan, India, Thailand, Egypt, Iraq, Ethiopia, Somalia and Israel.

On 10 December 1952 he wrote in his diary: "Bethlehem: Just the word is enough to fill my heart with emotion . . . I haven't been to the cave yet: I want to prepare myself a bit."

A few days later Nino and Poldo arrived (see note 3) and Carlo continued in his diary: "Christmas 1952. I spent the night in the cave which witnessed the divine mystery of the birth of Jesus. I heard the Holy Mass very near to the manger, and I felt that I was touching Jesus' hands. I felt Mary and Joseph near me. And with Christmas 1952, a new life: 6.30 wake up – 7-8 Mass (meditation first) – 9-13 work – 16-23 work – 23.30 examination and reflection – 24 rest . . ." (*Fondo Carretto/Jesus Caritas*.)

22. "I was thinking of getting married, and I had no idea that there could be another way for me.

"I met a doctor who told me about the Church and the beauty of serving it with one's whole being, yet staying in the world. I don't know what happened during those days or how it happened, but the fact is that while praying in an empty church, where I had gone to try and make some sense of the tumultuous thoughts raging through my mind, I heard the same voice which I had heard during confession with the old missionary: 'You will not get married; you will offer your life to me. I shall be your love for ever.'

"It was not difficult to give up marriage and to consecrate myself to God because everything had changed inside me; it would have felt strange to fall in love with a girl, because God filled my life so completely." (From *Lettere dal deserto*, La Scuola, Brescia, 1964, p. 6.)

JANUARY NOTES

1. "Jesus, angelic love – sweet song in the ear – marvellous honey in the mouth – heavenly nectar in the heart." (A hymn in the monastic antiphonary for the liturgy of the Holy Name of Jesus.)
2. "Holy Spirit, source of life, fire, love."
3. "All that is mine is yours" (Luke 15:31).
4. "Hidden God".

FEBRUARY NOTES

1. *Mario Fumagalli* (1931–88) came from Lombardy. As a Little Brother he spent time in a number of Fraternities in Belgium and France – and above all, in Japan. Having left the Little Brothers of Jesus under the auspices of the Opera Madonnina del Grappa, he became a Presbyter (1969) of the Church of Florence and carried out his pastoral ministry first as assistant parish priest in various parishes in the diocese, and later as parish priest in Petrazzi in the commune of Castelfiorentino. (See Appendix 6.)
2. *The Col of Géryville:* the natural caves between Géryville (see December 1954 note 11) and El-Abiodh, used by the Little Brothers to make retreats of varying length for purposes of prayer and solitude.
3. *Popol:* Paul Marnay (1929–82), a Little Brother from France, who died in a fire in Mexico City. He lived for a long time in student Fraternities, sharing his great erudition and profound knowledge of Hinduism with them.
4. *La Boulangerie:* baking. In a letter dated 7 March 1955, Carlo wrote: "Dear Father, this morning, after having studied at the University of Turin, after a career taking him to the top of Catholic Action and after speaking at thousands of conferences, your eldest son has finally done something worthwhile. Yes, Father mine, I made bread – white bread, well-risen 1-kg. loaves, well-kneaded, well-baked and crusty – just the way you like them. As you can see . . . I am going back to my origins and, while I stood by the stove, sweating and contented, I thought of the oven in front of the house in Camerana where, who knows how many times, you and your mother baked bread. Dear Mother, I wanted to tell you about my adventures in the kitchen, but now . . . it's all behind me. I have been promoted to baker. I was voted a good cook after a few days – thanks to you – and I handed over my duties to a Spaniard who has just arrived. Now when you eat bread, you will be able to think of your baker son . . ." (*Fondo Carretto/Jesus Caritas.*)
5. "Everything was done for him."

6. *Khaloua:* a pilgrimage, of about 500 kilometres from El-Abiodh to Béni Abbès, which the novices went on every February (see note 7). They covered 25-40 kilometres per day for 20 days, accompanied by an Arab guide and a number of camels carrying the big tent and food supplies. Departure was set for dawn after celebration of the Eucharist and a frugal breakfast of bread baked in the sand (*kesra*). A few dates provided refreshment during the morning march, which took place in complete silence. There was a very brief halt for a light meal at mid-day, and then they were *en route* again until sunset, when the big tent was pitched. Wood and twigs were collected for the fire and *couscous* was cooked for dinner. Then came vespers and compline, and so to sleep. This long walk was one of the most demanding periods in the novitiate; it ended with ten days spent in Charles de Foùcauld's hermitage in Béni Abbès. The return journey was by lorry along the track for motor traffic which runs through Bechar, Beni-Ounif and Ain-Sefra.

7. *Béni Abbès:* an Algerian oasis with thousands of palms and fruit trees and abundant water.

Here Charles de Foucauld opened his first Fraternity in 1901. The hermitage and the chapel, renovated in 1935, are still occupied by the Little Sisters of Jesus. The Little Brothers of the Gospel are also to be found at the oasis.

It was also here at Béni Abbès that in November 1955 the various Fraternities associated with Charles de Foucauld set up the Charles of Jesus Association, to consolidate the deep feeling of unity between them, while respecting their different vocations. (Charles of Jesus was Father de Foucauld's religious name.)

Cf. *Jesus Caritas*, the quarterly spiritual magazine of the Famiglia Charles de Foucauld, Abbazia di Sassovivo, 06034 Foligno, no. 20, October 1985.

8. Carlo was not able to continue with the pilgrimage, because of the worsening of a case of inflamed haemorrhoids.

MARCH NOTES
1. "Creator of heaven and earth."
2. *Mascara:* an Algerian town lying 600 metres above sea level; an important agricultural and commercial centre, well known for the manufacture of shoes and for its vineyards. Carlo went into hospital to have his haemorrhoids treated.

APRIL NOTES

1. "Those things which have always been acceptable."

MAY NOTES

1. "Without me you can do nothing."

2. The liturgical feast of Our Lady Help of Christians is celebrated with particular solemnity by the Salesians, the Order to which Dolce (Dolcidia) and Em (Emerenziana), two of Carlo's sisters, belong.

3. "The spring attracts he who is thirsty."

JUNE NOTES

1. "For he grew up before him like a young plant,
and like a root out of dry ground;
he had no form or majesty that we should look at him,
nothing in his appearance that we should desire him.
He was despised and rejected by others;
a man of suffering and acquainted with infirmity;
and as one from whom others hide their faces
he was despised, and we held him of no account."

(Isaiah 53:2–3)

AUGUST NOTES

1. *Domenico Tomaselli:* It has proved impossible to find out anything about this person. He was clearly badly in need of help, because Carlo even wrote and urged his family to take care of him.

2. The Italian version of the Lord's Prayer speaks of "Heavens" rather than "Heaven".

OCTOBER NOTES

1. See November note 1.

2. *Aunt Paola*, the sister-in-law of Carlo's mother, Maria. Paola was a member of the Rovea branch of the family, which came from Viola San Giorgio near Mondovi (in Cuneo province). Carlo's father's family came from Camerana (also in Cuneo). Carlo always remembered his origins with pride: "My family had its true roots deeply embedded in the Langhe hills, where my father and my mother were farmers, and had all the sweetness, strength and religious fervour of that wonderful part of the country in their blood" (from *Ho cercato e ho trovato*, Citadella, Assisi, 1983, p. 21).

NOVEMBER NOTES

1. "I wasn't feeling too well, and a nursing Brother who was fond of me and kept an affectionate eye on me was concerned and said to me: "Let me give you a course of injections, and you'll feel better, you'll see.'

" 'Go ahead,' I told him.

"So he, with all his loving care, injected a poison into my thigh which, in less than twenty-four hours, paralyzed my leg.

"He had made a mistake. He had picked up the wrong phial.

"Stupidly and, in my view, blamelessly, except that he was impulsive and thoughtless, he paralyzed my leg. I did not cry then, and I tried to be cheerful, if only to avoid sending the nursing Brother responsible out of his mind with grief. He was in a worse state than I was, both morally and emotionally. I was left lame." (From *Perché Signore?*, Morcelliana, Brescia, 1985, p. 11.)

Because of this accident Carlo was unable to go on the *khaloua* (see February note 6) *for the second time too*. He told his family about it in a letter written on 18 October 1955: "Dear ones, the *Khaloua*, or the pilgrimage to Béni Abbès, starts tomorrow . . . without me. I have to stay at headquarters to get through all my work, but principally because the Master of Novices wants me with him on the next one. Unfortunately I am becoming an important person here too!!! Luckily I have an excuse which teaches me humility: an injection of that stuff for snake-bite has made my leg swell a bit, and so I am glad of any excuse to put off the enormous strain of 600 kilometres on foot across the desert. I thought I had better write and give you the news straight away, because otherwise you . . . would stop writing to me for a month with the excuse that 'Muggins is out in the desert.' No, no, I am staying here, and you can write to me without delay . . ." (*Fondo Carretto/Jesus Caritas.*)

Brother René Voillaume gives this account of the incident: "Brother Carlo wasn't able to go on this long walk because one of his legs was paralyzed. His infirmity was caused by a mistake on the part of the nursing Brother who, to treat his influenza, gave him an intramuscular injection from a phial intended to be given orally, not injected. What's more, the injection was given badly and he touched a nerve in the leg. Sometimes Carlo mentions his disability, which is often painful, but always with discretion, and he never says what caused it, or blames the Brother whose mistake was responsible for this trial which marked him for life. For Carlo this paralysis was a real and mysterious visitation from God. It was like Jacob being touched on the hip by the angel after a night of wrestling with God (Genesis 32:25-26). At the outset of his novitiate, Carlo had told me of his ambition to dedicate his religious life as a Little Brother to working as a guide in the mountains, so he could save climbers in difficulties. He had to give up any idea of this sort for good: Providence had other plans for him."

2. "I was forty-four when it happened; and it was the most serious call of my life: the call to the contemplative life . . . This time I had to say yes without understanding a thing: 'Leave everything. I don't want your work any longer – I want your prayer, your love.' It was the decisive call. And I never understood it better than that evening at vespers on the feast-day of St Charles, 1954, when I said yes to the Voice.

" 'Come with me to the desert. There is something greater than your work: prayer. There is a more effective power than your words: love!'

"Without having read the Constitutions of the Little Brothers of Jesus, I joined their congregation; without knowing anything about Charles de Foucauld I joined his following." (From *Lettere dal deserto*, La Scuola editrice, Brescia, 1964, pp. 7-8.)

3. *Pietro Carretto* (b. 1912) went to Thailand as a Salesian probationer when he was only sixteen. He was ordained in 1939, and after holding various posts in his congregation he was consecrated bishop in 1951. Today he is bishop emeritus of the diocese of Surat Thani.

4. *Antonio:* Anton Ho (b. 1930), one of the first Vietnamese Little Brothers. He spent about ten years in voluntary imprisonment in Bellechasse Prison in Switzerland.

5. "Deal with me according to your word."

NOTES TO APPENDIX 2

1. *Charles de Foucauld* was born in Strasbourg on 15 September 1858, to a rich and aristocratic family.

Orphaned when they were very young, he and his sister Maria were brought up by their paternal grandfather. Charles chose a military career because he preferred a life of pleasure and dissipation to one of study. But in the end, pride and a spirit of adventure won the day, and he became an exemplary soldier.

A dangerous "exploration of Morocco" (1883-84) won him a testimonial from the Société de Géographie. An attack of spiritual malaise overwhelmed him in these Muslim surroundings, and he was helped with wisdom and tenderness by his cousin Maria de Bondy (1850-1934). It led him to the confessional of Abbe Henry Huvelin (1838-1910) in the church of St Augustine in Paris. After a pilgrimage to the Holy Land (1889), he joined the Trappists (1890–96) and was sent to a poor priory in Syria. He left it for good (1897) to go and live in Nazareth, lodging with the Poor Clares, where he lived in imitation of his "beloved brother and Lord, Jesus". He became a priest in 1901, and set out on his Saharan adventure in Algeria: first in Béni Abbès and then in Tamanrasset. He was killed at dusk on 1 December 1916. A French viscount, he became the poorest of the poor, a seeker for God in the desert like the early Fathers, but he was also enamoured of a mankind redeemed by the blood of Christ. He became a contemplative and the prototype of the evangelical missionary of the twentieth century.

Cf. Jean-Francois Six, *Itinerario Spirituale di Charles de Foucauld*, Morcelliana, Brescia, 1961; Marguerite Castillon du Perron, *Charles de Foucauld*, Jaca Book, Milan, 1986.

2. The Church only awards the name of "founder", in the exact sense of the word, to one who has gathered disciples during his lifetime, and who, having lived a certain kind of life in their company, passes on to them a rule duly approved by the Church itself. This approval, which constitutes foundation in the strict sense, is given only after a period of trial. For this reason Rome refused to consider Charles de Foucauld as a "founder" when the Constitutions of the Fraternity of El-Abiodh-Sidi-Cheikh were examined in 1936.

3. This was written during the winter of 1932–33. The original refers to two great texts by Pius XI: the Apostolic Constitution "Umbratilem" (addressed to the Carthusians, 1924); and the "Rerum Ecclesiae" Encyclical (on the way in which missions should evolve, 1926).

4. The same which was to spark off the 'rebellion' of a certain lieutenant of de Foucauld's, who had been expelled from the ranks of the army a few months earlier "for notoriously bad conduct".

5. *From the Sahara to the Whole World*, the title of Little Sister Madeleine de Jésus' first volume of memoirs. The expansion of the Fraternity during this period is described in the second volume, *Da un capo all'altro del mondo*, Città Nuova, Rome, 1983.

NOTES TO APPENDIX 4

1. The Little Sister relates: "Milad stood up half way through the Office. I hesitated a bit; but then he gestured to me that he needed me to follow him. When we reached his room he told me: 'I have a terrible pain in my chest.' He gave me his instruments to examine him with (it was, I

believe, the first time in fifteen years). I immediately gave him two injections; he himself showed me where to find the alcohol, the file for the ampoules, the tourniquet and so forth. I said to him: 'Perhaps it would be better if you got back into bed, Milad. I'm going to call Raymond to give you a hand . . .' And I went to get Brother Raymond. When we got back to the room he was standing against the wall with closed eyes, and his face had changed. We laid him down on his bed . . . It happened in the time it took me to fetch Brother Raymond . . . It all happened so fast, so simply. We left the chapel at 7.15; at 7.40 Milad had left us . . . For me his death is the image of his life. Milad was very simple and rarely thought of himself . . . A few months before he had told me: 'Stop looking at yourself. Look at God and look at others.' " (From *Les Petits Frères de Jésus, nouvelles periodiques pour les amis des Fraternités, no.* 101, 1985.)